PRAISE FOR *FINDING PEACE WHEN YOUR HEART IS IN PIECES*

"Paul Coleman takes the reader on a journey through grief and healing as one who knows both. This touching and insightful book is a must read for anyone trying to find peace in the sea of sorrow left by death."

—Mark Anthony, author of *Never Letting Go: Heal Grief with Help from the Other Side*

"In *Finding Peace When Your Heart Is in Pieces*, Dr. Paul Coleman invites readers to explore the peace behind the pain of loss, the harmony that lies within struggle, and the wonder of the work itself. His ability to help others connect the emotional and intuitive dots is a gift to all."

—Debra Snyder, PhD, author of *Intuitive Parenting: Listening to the Wisdom of Your Heart* (Atria/Beyond Words 2010)

"Paul Coleman's important new book *Finding Peace When Your Heart Is in Pieces* helps you remove the dark veil on your thoughts and realize that even when the past cannot be changed, YOU can be transformed."

—Jarek Zabczynski, director/producer of Jester Pictures, winner for Best Music Video at the 2011 Las Vegas Film Festival (Director); winner, BET Award for Best Inspirational Video 2010 (Director)

PRAISE FOR *FINDING PEACE WHEN YOUR HEART IS IN PIECES*

"*Finding Peace When Your Heart Is in Pieces* is a practical, loving, and needed guide for anyone seeking to forge an internal roadmap toward peace and forgiveness after loss. Paul Coleman co-pilots the reader's GPS from chaos to contentment, while honoring their human experience."

—Austyn Wells, spiritual medium

"Paul Coleman's *Finding Peace When Your Heart Is in Pieces* illuminates brand new insights of hope and compassion to help guide you through life's difficult losses and transitions."

—Lora Lee Ecobelli, actor (Broadway and Off-Broadway), screenwriter, and Artistic Director of Blue Horse Repertory Company

"*Finding Peace When Your Heart Is in Pieces* is a much-needed book during current times of stress, loss, and upheaval. Dr. Paul Coleman offers readers an oasis in the midst of personal storms."

—Athena A. Drewes, author of *Integrative Play Therapy* (Wiley, 2011); director of Clinical Training, Astor Services for Children and Families; periodic contributor to A&E's *Psychic Kids*

"When we struggle to find answers to life's challenges, *Finding Peace When Your Heart Is in Pieces* and Dr. Paul Coleman's other books always provide a 'right on' resource."

—Ron Mombello, TV writer (*I Love Lucy, Kate & Allie, Hollywood Squares*), film critic ("On the Aisle with Ron Mombello"), and author of *iRage: Behind the Wheel*

Finding Peace When Your Heart Is in Pieces

Finding Peace When Your Heart Is in Pieces

A Step-by-Step Guide to the Other Side of Grief, Loss, and Pain

PAUL COLEMAN, PSYD

Avon, Massachusetts

6048673 .

Published by
Adams Media, a division of F+W Media, Inc.
57 Littlefield Street, Avon, MA 02322. U.S.A.
www.adamsmedia.com

ISBN 10: 1-4405-7338-7
ISBN 13: 978-1-4405-7338-5
eISBN 10: 1-4405-7339-5
eISBN 13: 978-1-4405-7339-2

Printed in the United States of America.

10   9   8   7   6   5   4   3   2   1

Library of Congress Cataloging-in-Publication Data

Coleman, Paul,
  Finding peace when your heart is in pieces / Paul Coleman, PsyD.
    pages cm
  Includes index.
  ISBN 978-1-4405-7338-5 (pb) -- ISBN 1-4405-7338-7 (pb) -- ISBN 978-1-4405-7339-2 (ebook) -- ISBN 1-4405-7339-5 (ebook)
  1. Self-actualization (Psychology) 2. Optimism. I. Title.
  BF637.S4.C6523 2015
  155.9'3--dc23
                                    2014015637

Many of the designations used by manufacturers and sellers to distinguish their product are claimed as trademarks. Where those designations appear in this book and F+W Media, Inc. was aware of a trademark claim, the designations have been printed with initial capital letters.

Client stories are true, but names and other details have been changed to protect confidentiality.

This book is intended as general information only, and should not be used to diagnose or treat any health condition. In light of the complex, individual, and specific nature of health problems, this book is not intended to replace professional medical advice. The ideas, procedures, and suggestions in this book are intended to supplement, not replace, the advice of a trained medical professional. Consult your physician before adopting any of the suggestions in this book, as well as about any condition that may require diagnosis or medical attention. The author and publisher disclaim any liability arising directly or indirectly from the use of this book.

Cover design by Jessica Pooler.
Cover image © Ariadna De Raadt/123RF.

This book is available at quantity discounts for bulk purchases.
For information, please call 1-800-289-0963.

For Claire

CONTENTS

ACKNOWLEDGMENTS

No book of mine would ever have been possible without the expertise of Patricia and Michael Snell of the Michael Snell Literary Agency. And a special thanks to Patricia Snell for her unwavering dedication in helping me shape the book proposal over many months of hard work, and for her line-by-line editing prowess which helped me fine-tune the final manuscript and make it shine. Pat and Mike, I am forever grateful for your professionalism, talents, wisdom, enthusiasm, and friendship. Every writer should be so fortunate.

Thanks to Maria Ribas, Laura Daly, Brendan O'Neill, and the talented production staff at Adams Media for their dedication to this book and their continued faith in me as an author.

A special thank you to Jarek Zabczynski of Jester Pictures (*www.jesterpictures.com*) for his outstanding work in creating the video book trailer. It isn't every writer who can call a national award winning director/producer a good friend.

I am grateful for the time and immense talents of the actors, crew, and all who helped in any way in the production of the video book trailer. It is no small feat. Thanks to Kevin Barnes, Anna Coleman, Jody Coleman, Luke Coleman, Ryan Katzer, Jen Mille, Bentley Creighton O'Reilly, Anna Marie Paolercio, Amy Schaffer, Kat Scicluna, Charlie Scrivner, Nancy Scrivner, CarolAnn Smith, Jeff Smith, AnnChris Warren, Eli Wells, Jeff Wilson, Douglas Woolley, and Julie Woolley.

Thanks to County Players Falls Theater for allowing the use of their stage for the video shoot. And a special thank you to Peter and Bernice Edman. Your unswerving dedication to bringing high-quality theater to the Hudson Valley for over fifty years has blessed us all.

Writing can be a lonely process, but my closest friends have always been nearby, encouraging me, inspiring me, and making life just plain old fun! I can't thank Ryan Katzer, Jen Mille, and Rick Meyer enough for their love and friendship, and for making the second half of my life very entertaining. And a special thanks to Equity actor Ryan Katzer and to Jen Mille for your artistic talents, sacrifices, professionalism, and devotion to making my stage play *The Foot Shooters* a highlight of the last five years.

Many thanks to Ron Mombello, writer and friend, who has always been willing to read and critique any manuscript I place in front of him. Breakfast soon, Ron.

Special thanks to Jim Harris for his enthusiasm and encouragement for all of my endeavors and for his ever-ready humor. I always look forward to our Friday morning chats. And a special shout-out to Tabinda Magsood for her welcoming smile and for keeping Jim in line.

A hearty thanks to Cindy Franze and MaryAnn Dysard-Iversen for their unfaltering support of my work, for organizing the monthly group meetings, and for preparing the coffee and delicious baked goods. Thanks also to Steven Amendola for the use of his salon for those meetings.

I've attended a number of training workshops that have made a big difference both in my personal life and in my understanding of the survival of consciousness after physical death. In particular I wish to thank the Reverend Janet Nohavec, John Holland, and James Van Praagh for their many remarkable workshops I've attended. Most especially in this regard, I wish to thank mediums Robert Brown and Ann Burbedge of England for their wisdom, kindness, friendship, and lifelong dedication to showing others that goodbyes are not forever.

Many thanks to Vanora St. Clair for her insightful thoughts and comments when my book was in its early stages of development, and most important of all for her friendship.

Thanks to Claire, Ann, Jane, Deb, and John—my forever companions on this journey of life. Better siblings there could never be.

Whenever I need inspiration, I need look no further than to my children. Luke, Anna, and Julia continue to do remarkable things with their lives, always creative, always in service of others, always with joy, enthusiasm, and determination. And thanks forever and always to my wife Jody for this amazing and joyous life we have co-created. I love you all.

INTRODUCTION

The Journey from Pain to Peace

"I do not want the peace which passeth understanding, I want the understanding which bringeth peace."

—HELEN KELLER

—— Finding Peace Together ——

The early January blizzard had blasted us through the night. The next morning the sidewalks lay buried under nearly two feet of snow. As the below-zero wind-chill stung us, my mother and siblings followed single file in a solemn procession through the cemetery to lay my beloved Dad to rest. The nearby headstones barely peeked out above the windblown drifts. The priest shivered uncontrollably. The wind moaned like a cello. In a flash it was over. We then trudged our way back to our cars, my mom dazed and forlorn, back to a family home that never felt quite the same after Dad died.

Nighttime approached, the streetlights blinked on, and I stepped outside to shovel. The air was still, the neighborhood serene. A lone string of stars—twinkling like a leftover strand of Christmas tree lights—hovered high above us and eons away in the otherwise pitch-black sky. The cold air took my breath away. Road crews had pushed a four-foot-high mountain of heavy packed snow in front of our driveway, so I now began the exhausting task of reducing the mountain to a molehill. My brother soon showed up to help. An hour later, with a second wind, we walked up the nearby hill and began shoveling our neighbor's driveway.

At first I assumed we were simply being neighborly. But soon I realized our deeper motivation: we needed to work the shovel to symbolically bury our Dad. It seemed the right and honorable thing to do, to wield our shovels, strain our backs, and exhaust our bodies. Just as the pain of childbirth is the price paid to bring life into this world—pain born of love—we suffer pain as we send loved ones off from this world into the next. In between birth and death are the roads we travel on this sometimes painful, sometimes glorious, but always remarkable journey we call "life."

The Road Ahead

Enduring a painful loss is one of the most difficult challenges we all face in life. At its core, a loss creates a void, a hole in your life that must be faced. Losses come in all shapes and sizes—the death of a loved one, a permanent injury, a debilitating illness, a relationship breakup, unemployment. As you begin to live your life with this void, you likely experience myriad feelings, among them sadness, anger, hopelessness, and fear. The overwhelming pain of a loss disrupts your everyday life and can even make you question your place on earth. This pain can seem endless, and you might feel that you'll never know inner peace again. But no matter what happens in your outer world, inner peace is possible. When a significant event turns your world upside down, you will embark on a transformational journey. This journey is unavoidable and part of the human condition. In your life you will meet with triumphs but also, undoubtedly, with great trials after which you will never be quite the same. And the journey never ends, not really, for you must always evolve. You will learn much about yourself—come face to face with your strengths, your weaknesses, and facets of yourself you barely knew existed. You will arrive at pathways along the road—choicepoints—that will lead you to either inner peace or pain. Which paths will you choose? How fully will your life evolve? My hope is that, when faced with life's inevitable losses, burdens, injustices, and mysteries, you will accept with courage what *can't* be changed as you accept with determination and grit what *must* be changed. My hope is that you will embrace all of what life has to offer—the good and the bad—in such a way that the losses in life don't break your spirit, your trust, your faith—or your heart.

You will discover the deeper peace that can be found along your journey—no matter how much you doubt such peace is possible. There are many useful books that help you to "cope with" or "learn to live with" loss. This book is different. It reveals how fear keeps your pain alive and that a special bridge exists that, when crossed over, allows you to experience inner peace even when your loss is profound. You will encounter that bridge along your personal journey. It is one of the Four Paths of Transformation that will enlighten, inspire, and guide you along your journey. But those paths have their counterparts that, if traveled, will leave you stranded with fear. Which pathways you choose will determine whether or not you find inner peace. This book aims to raise your level of awareness as to who you really are and what your life is really all about. As such, it will speak of things you *need* to hear when the things you *want* to hear aren't always forthcoming. I hope it will help you to experience these deeper truths: that a peaceful heart is possible even with profound loss; that your life still has purpose and meaning; and goodbyes are not forever.

Is it true that everything happens for a reason? It can be comforting for some to believe that a greater purpose exists for why a loss had to be endured. But for others, no underlying purpose could ever justify such a profound loss. If you connect all the dots in your life, you may discover that certain early experiences foreshadowed both the challenges you now face and how you will respond to them. And years from now when you look back upon your hardships, you may view them from a wiser perspective, seeing the sweet as well as the bitter. It is often only in retrospect, if ever, that we understand the significance of some events and why they unfolded the way they did. As you embark on your journey, you will not be able to see how and where it will all end or what the underlying purposes might be, what we might call the mysteries of life. There will always be a bend in the road you cannot see past. Always. But don't make hasty judgments. What looks like a dead end may instead be a place of hope and healing. Things are not always as they appear.

You are not alone. We will take this journey together. We will walk step by step and this book will light the way. Come take the *first step* with me.

CHAPTER 1

The Heroic Journey

"All journeys have secret destinations
of which the traveler is unaware."

—MARTIN BUBER

—— Finding Peace Together ——

As Tuesday morning dawned, Jenny woke early, pulled on her favorite shorts and the new T-shirt she had bought the day before, and laced up her running shoes to take a brisk walk. Later she would take the train north to Dutchess County to resume her nursing classes. Smiling, she thought to herself that she had never seen the sky so clear or so blue. But when she strolled by the World Trade Center, she heard a noise very different from the usual city sounds—a deafening roar. Looking up, she saw that a plane had flown into one of the World Trade Center's Twin Towers. She and other stunned onlookers watched as debris began falling, seriously injuring many below. Jenny's instincts took over. Without thinking of her own safety, the second-year nursing student immediately ran to help. She volunteered to assist the professional medics who quickly arrived at the scene, offering encouragement, kind words, and simple first-aid to the wounded while relaying information to the medics.

"Where's my wife? Is she okay?" an elderly man with a bleeding face frantically called to Jenny. "I can't find her!"

"My friend is unconscious!" another man cried out. "Help her!"

There were too many to count. Some had been innocently walking into the building to go to work, but many more flooded out of the building now billowing with smoke and fire.

"Everyone started shouting and screaming at once," Jenny told me later. She raced to those who appeared mildly injured, asking them to sit and wait for assistance. Medics were placing some people with serious injuries on flat boards to prevent further damage, their heads and torsos immobilized in restraints. Jenny spoke to them, offering the calm reassurance that they would soon get the help they needed. In those first frantic moments, no one could have imagined that another plane would hit the second tower. No one could have imagined that the towers would collapse. Neither Jenny nor any of the medical personnel could have imagined how they would have no choice but to run for their lives, leaving behind those, only seconds before, they had so desperately tried to help. Among the victims were those tethered to the flat boards, unable to free themselves, unable to save themselves.

"I should have realized those towers would fall. If I had, those people might be alive today," Jenny told me months later, tears streaming down her face. Haunted by guilt, Jenny had come to me for help. Little did she know she was beginning her journey through loss. Like so many suffering loss, Jenny showed symptoms such as intrusive memories, sleep disturbance, crying spells, a sense of detachment from the world, and a preoccupation with self-blame. Logic told her one thing, that no one could have anticipated the awful turn of events. Her emotions told her she was at fault.

Fortunately, over time Jenny came to accept what had happened and no longer blamed herself. Her heart had found peace.

Finding a Peaceful Heart

When you experience deep loss, your heart remembers how things used to be and does not easily give way to the changes it must accept. Everything looks askew. Everything feels wrong. Yet somehow your heart goes on. No, your broken heart will never be the same. But that's not supposed to be the outcome, anyway. A peaceful heart, the heroic heart, embraces what was good and loving about what once was and then opens up a space there to receive more *from* life and to offer more *to* life. The inner peace I am writing about need not be found in sacred sanctuaries. It waits in all the ordinary places if you know how to look. Sometimes peace may show up in fleeting moments of sweet serenity when you smile at some beautiful, bittersweet memory. Those moments are signposts for something more enduring. They reveal what is already there—joy, gratitude, tranquility, and love. They need only be resurrected. You will be outraged at the loss until you surrender to your reality. And therein lies your chance to heal. In healing, you come to accept that things have permanently changed but know that it is possible to peacefully coexist with life's givens—inevitable losses, devastating injuries, dashed hopes, painful estrangements, tearful goodbyes . . . . When you

make peace with loss, your suffering lessens considerably and your gratitude for your life expands.

Early Reactions to Loss

You will know you have yet to make peace with loss when you:

- Struggle to accept what cannot be changed.
- Begin recovery but too slowly and painfully.
- Find annoyance with the "little things."
- Take things too personally.
- Possess much but know "something is missing."
- Recall painful childhood memories too often.
- Pose unanswerable questions about senseless, tragic situations.
- See yourself as a victim and life as unfair.

One of the most rewarding comments I hear my clients make is this: "I never thought about it that way before!" I hope you will look at your problems and losses in a completely new way as you read this book. Doing so automatically causes your pain to diminish and sometimes to disintegrate entirely. Do your mind and your thoughts filling your head lead you to happiness or disappointment? Love or hate? Inner peace or anger, guilt, shame, or misery? Peaceful relationships or contentious ones? Are you jealous of others who have what you no longer have? If so, you're still in the process of healing. When you possess a peaceful heart, you do not reflexively find fault with others or yourself. You aim to understand more than to judge. And you accept—peacefully, not grudgingly—that some situations or people cannot change and that the losses that occurred may never be recovered.

Look Inside Yourself

Judy, raised by harsh, critical parents, never felt good enough and still to this day becomes deeply hurt and frustrated when one of her parents finds fault with her.

"Why can't they appreciate me?" Judy asked. "How do I get them to change?"

Judy mistakenly believed that her heart would only find peace if her parents spoke lovingly to her. But until she discovered ways to peacefully accept that she never received from her parents what she had most wanted, and until she could recognize her own value without needing her parents' validation, she would remain unhappy and insecure.

We often make the mistake of attributing our lack of inner peace to conditions out of our control—a world in turmoil, a relationship that has ended or is in conflict, or a goal thwarted. But peace is an inside job. When it happens, it happens *within* regardless of what is happening *without*. The heroic heart cultivates gratitude even in the midst of suffering. It finds glory in the inglorious; beauty in the less than beautiful. It accepts life's ups and downs, heartaches, disappointments, and inevitable losses.

The inner peace cultivated by a heroic heart is not the same as fleeting happiness, that which comes and goes. It is not merely a feeling of being relaxed or that nondescript "feeling better." Peace of heart is a deeper sense of lasting contentment. It is a sweet feeling, sometimes accompanied by sadness, but a feeling of serenity despite what is happening in your life. It is the kind of tranquility that allows the pains of life to peacefully coexist with all that has been joyous, all that has left you with gratitude, and all that deserves to be lovingly held and remembered.

This book—this journey with its Four Paths of Transformation—will help you achieve that feeling.

The Forces That Shape Us

If you look back upon your life, you will notice that the people and events that most influenced you fall into two categories. First are those forces that were part of your regular, daily life (family, friends, schools attended, towns lived in, personal strengths, physical limitations, and so forth). Second are those forces that appeared randomly or unexpectedly (chance meetings, sudden accidents, unforeseen opportunities, unplanned decisions). Most people can truthfully say, "Had I never happened to be in a certain place at a certain time, I never would have _____." Many such "happenstances" change lives permanently.

When I applied to the graduate school I most wanted to attend, Purdue University, I did not get accepted. It was a disappointing blow. Yet the school I did attend, Central Michigan University, was where I met my wife, and we have been happily married for thirty years. I cannot imagine my life without her or without our children. At the time, getting accepted into Purdue University was something I deeply wanted. Thank goodness I did not get what I wanted. Of course, a "rational" cynic might claim that had I gone to school elsewhere, I might still be happy. I can't argue with the logic. But by that same reasoning, had I gone to a different school and lived elsewhere, many unfortunate things may have happened to me.

It comes down to this: Do you believe that our lives are influenced by a combination of free will plus pure chance, or that our lives are also influenced and guided by forces unseen? Later chapters will discuss that idea more fully, but for now please keep in mind that our rational mind is limited. We may impress ourselves with our intelligence and logic, but rarely do we know enough information to be able to say for certain "why" things happen the way they do. Open up to the possibility that more is going on behind the scenes as you stand center stage in your life. This allows for inner peace to emerge even in times of loss and pain.

The Path to Peace

As you seek a more tranquil heart, you must loosen up some of the bindings that have restricted you, the fears and beliefs that have made inner peace harder to obtain. Sometimes we see just the momentary snapshots, failing to see the panoramic picture that will unfold over time. How you respond to a tragedy, loss, or injustice ultimately determines how exactly it will impact your life. A tragedy where no lessons are learned, where no compassion follows, is merely stand-alone suffering and is even more tragic. But if you can create meaning for that suffering, you may escape despair. *The meanest form of suffering is suffering with no meaning.*

The Heroic Journey Is Not a Straight Path

What we might ordinarily think of as a desirable outcome sometimes instead leads us down an undesirable road. The old adage "Be careful what you wish for—you might just get it" reminds us that we do not always know what is in our best interest. We view some things as good that turn out bad, and we view some things as bad that turn out good. If you could plot the course of your life on a graph, you would discover that the path from point A to a long-desired point B was not always a straight line. In between those two points, all manner of things happened to you that contributed to where you are—and who you are—today.

Reducing Stress Is Not the Same as Inner Peace

Another mistaken idea is that deep inner peace can be experienced only if you live a life of spiritual or religious devotion accompanied by deprivation—fewer possessions, less money, more sacrifice, a general letting go of the things that might make life pleasurable and fun. It is the subconscious reason why many people settle for "relaxation exercises" or "keeping busy" when seeking to alleviate emotional pain. Inner peace is then replaced by mere stress reduction or mindless distractions. It may be helpful but it is also superficial. The problem is that lightweight efforts at finding true inner peace—cheery thoughts, better diets, new hobbies, or anger management—buckle under the load of real suffering and loss.

What Is a Peaceful Heart?

To make peace with loss, you must cultivate peace in your heart. That is a challenge when your heart is broken, but it *is* achievable, because we are built to experience peace.

A peaceful heart:

1. Seeks simplicity, where life is not driven by either deprivation or accumulation.

2. Lets go of anxieties and false beliefs that we cling to as life preservers but that are actually fear preservers.
3. Knows that the things let go will cost little, that peace is incompatible with a need to cling.
4. Looks within itself, without judgment. Therein lies a deeper understanding.
5. Makes peace with uncertainty; knows that it does not know all.

Setting Out on Your Heroic Journey

Certain timeless stories by Charles Dickens, Jane Austen, and William Shakespeare, along with the Greek classics and the more recent *Lord of the Rings, Star Wars,* and *Harry Potter,* resonate within us because they reveal greater truths. Western civilization's greatest stories and the lives of history's greatest people share something in common: they are tales of people on a quest, one they usually did not ask for, who overcome obstacles and loss and become more than they ever thought they could be. They have embarked on what Joseph Campbell has called "the hero's journey."

We are all on a quest, whether or not we realize it: to seek greater wisdom, to experience love, and to prevent or heal suffering. We are on our own hero's journey to find inner peace in the face of life's givens. When we must face the hardships accompanying great challenges or great loss, our journey is not that different from Frodo's journey in *The Lord of the Rings,* or from the boy wizard's journey in *Harry Potter.*

Like Frodo and Harry at the beginning of their sagas:

• You see life as predictable, with everything proceeding as it always has been.

- You are thrown off course unexpectedly by some major event and now face a new road, a new journey.
- You refuse the quest initially, fearing the unknown.
- You choose to accept the journey, reluctantly, discovering you have no alternative.
- You seek guidance from wise mentors—priests, wizards, sages, God—and perhaps your own intuition.
- You cross the threshold into a world that seems vastly different from your ordinary world, with unfamiliar rules.
- You are tested along the way, facing your greatest fears and reaching inside of yourself to bring out strengths you did not know you possessed.
- You return to your old world a different person, seeing that old world differently and gaining a deeper understanding. Others may not understand you but you move forward with peace. *You are illuminated.*

We have all faced those challenges. We have all had difficult choices to make. Your own hero's journey as you grapple with loss need not be the stuff of great novels. Still, it requires great courage to, for example, raise children alone after a spouse dies unexpectedly. It requires great courage to persevere with optimism when faced with a life-threatening illness. It requires great courage to rise to greater spiritual heights after falling into doubt and despair.

The Importance of Transforming

Make no mistake, the changes you will make and lessons you will learn will not bring you back to where you were before calamity struck. Your life is forever altered. You will now view your world from a perspective that is more wise and peaceful, or one more cynical and sad. If you limit your efforts to only superficial changes, any hardships faced will be mismanaged, any lessons learned will be trite, any losses suffered will be meaningless. You may get through them but you won't rise above them. Most of us can, at least for a while, grit our teeth and bear what we must bear. Endurance may build muscle, but it does not heal.

Endurance is not transformation. But transformation endures.

Transformation Is Part of Healing

It takes courage to seek inner peace so that life's losses will not defeat you. A loss may actually inspire you—and if you are inspired despite defeat, it was not a true defeat after all. You will discover how true transformation requires you to act with a more profound purpose and perceive events from a higher ledge on your journey up the mountain. The next chapter will help you understand where you are now—the level that you operate from most of the time—in the hope that it will clarify where you need to move forward. Making peace with loss is a key to that transformation. *And here is the part to remember: transformation will challenge you but resistance to transformation will wear you down, sustain misery, and further complicate your life.*

Resistance to Transformation Is Futile

Not everyone initially approaches transformation with an open mind and an open heart. Linda had no interest in transforming herself. She preferred stability to change, even if that stability made her miserable. She would find a way to cope with it—often saying that while her life had its problems, at least it was predictable. She knew that her quiet, unassuming husband had fallen out of love with her and that her son, struggling to stay off drugs, was for the moment clean and sober. Then out of the blue, her life went into a tailspin. Her husband suddenly walked out, taking most of their joint bank account with him. Her mother suffered a stroke, and her job was in jeopardy to layoffs. She wanted medication to help her cope and was nostalgic for the "good old days," preferring them to a chaotic present and an unknown future.

Linda did not want transformation at first—but she needed to understand that her life was being transformed *whether she wanted it to or not*. The structure of her outer life would never be the same. Life does that to us sometimes. We get hit by one blow, and sometimes barely catch our breath before another one strikes.

Linda soon realized that fixing her life by practical means—hiring a divorce attorney, getting her son into a rehab facility, finding someone to care for her mother—was necessary, but was not the whole picture. Learning to merely cope would not be enough. That's what she had always done—choosing a path that led to stagnation rather than transformation. She had become an expert at getting by. But now it was time to let go of old ways and look at her life—and her future—through new eyes. That's the way to a peaceful heart.

The Four Paths

If you have suffered a painful loss, then the journey you did not ask for has begun. The first crossroad is about to appear. One road leads to a dead end. That is the road where you shake your fist and ask, "Why?" On that road you beg, "Make this go away!" It is your Gethsemane moment when you plead with God or the universe to reverse what has happened. Most of us go down that road at least some bit of distance when we are very afraid or in deep mourning.

This book will help you turn yourself around and choose to take the other road. That road, though challenging, offers a way through your suffering to the other side of grief.

Awaiting you on that road is the light at the end of your loss.

On that road you will encounter four separate paths, each with a different lesson for achieving inner peace. If you do not select these paths, then by default you will walk along their counterparts—paths that will only take you into deeper despair and greater cynicism. There is no option to sidestep your journey. Your journey is inevitable and has in fact already begun. I have found that traveling even one of the healing paths can add a significant amount of peace to a heart. But to fully make peace with loss and to strengthen your ability to come to terms with any future losses, do what you can to walk all four healing pathways.

When you walk all four paths you will not only experience inner peace for yourself, you will gain the capacity to help others make peace with their loss and to heal. Maybe assisting others is not a goal for you right now. Maybe it's all you can do just to get out of bed in the morning and start your day. That's okay. Then again, if other family members are suffering through the same loss as you are, how you cope will always affect them. *You will learn you can only achieve in your outer world what has already been achieved in your inner world.*

The four pathways are these:

The Path of Acceptance

This is the foundational pathway. Its counterpart is the Path of Resistance. When you emotionally accept reality, you can begin to change what you are capable of changing and let be what cannot be changed. Suffering comes when we resist life's givens. Acceptance is neither approval nor denial, but is saying "Yes" to reality, to what is. This pathway offers us *the energy of joyful humility.*

The Path of Inspiration

This is the pathway that compels you to pursue the mysteries behind your everyday existence and look beyond your everyday notion of reality to that which may, in fact, be more substantial. Its counterpart is the Path of Illusion. While you may or may not believe in an afterlife or believe in God, the Path of Inspiration compels you to examine more deeply what you may not see but is there—your spirituality. This pathway offers us *the energy of mystical wisdom.*

The Path of Release

This pathway shows you how believing in a positive future—one you may not see yet—fosters inner peace. Its counterpart is the Path of Despair. By learning to release doubt and fear, you begin to peacefully coexist with uncertainty and stop trying to control all outcomes. This pathway offers us *the energy of patient trust.*

The Path of Compassion

This pathway is the will to act with benevolence, generosity, and forgiveness toward yourself and others. Its counterpart is the Path of Emptiness. Whereas the other three pathways involve an inward focus, compassion requires an outward deed. You must *act* with compassion, not merely *feel* compassionate. Compassion allows you to move *away* from yourself and *toward* others in acts of service. Compassionate acts provide perspective. They reveal how your life is inextricably bound to the lives of others, and that in giving, you will receive. This pathway offers *the energy of unifying love.*

The Power of the Paths

These pathways contain hidden aspects you may never have considered before. They all contain ideas, insights, and paradoxes that will open you up to a new way of seeing the world—both the visible and the invisible world.

If you take the time to contemplate what these ideas have to offer and begin to apply them to your life, you will discover that *suffering from loss need not break your spirit, but your spirit can indeed break your suffering.*

CHAPTER 2

The Awakening

"A single event can awaken within us
a stranger totally unknown to us."

—ANTOINE DE SAINT-EXUPÉRY

—— Finding Peace Together ——

On his best days, Jack presented an imposing image: over six feet tall with exceptionally broad shoulders, biceps as large as an average man's thighs, hands like shovels. At age forty-six, he was "as fit as a fiddle" and determined to stay that way. In fact, his goal was to stay as fit as he was twenty-five years earlier when he was newly enlisted in the U.S. Army. Physically, he was the picture of health and confidence. But in my office on the day we met, he sat slumped and quivering. He tried repeatedly but was at a loss to explain why he suddenly became so deeply depressed, nearly suicidal, over so minor an incident.

It had been his regular visitation day with his seven-year-old son, Davey. As Davey ran up the driveway, Jack threw him a long pass with the football. Little Davey made the catch but tripped, falling face-first on the pavement, knocking out a baby tooth and suffering a big swollen lip in the process.

"It looked worse than it was," Jack said quietly. "But something happened inside me. I felt responsible for his injury, guilty for having caused it. I couldn't stop crying. I had to call my ex to pick him up. I took the week off from work and stayed in bed the whole time. I'm falling apart and I don't know why. *Please help me.*"

I asked Jack about his background. All seemed routine until he spoke of his time in Afghanistan. It was 1988 and the Soviets were fighting Afghan rebels. The United States and our allies were providing the Afghan rebels with weapons and tactical military assistance. As Jack watched the carefully planned military maneuvers through binoculars, an unsuspecting regiment of Russian soldiers was ambushed and killed by weapons he helped to supply.

"I'm proud of my country," he said, his eyes rimmed with red. "But it wasn't our war. I thought about how all those soldiers all had families, parents, siblings, wives, and children just like we did. Some were younger than me. It was horrible." He paused and said "I deserve to be punished."

Jack went on to work very hard in therapy to finally overcome his depression. When he "awakened," he connected the dots of his adult life, the failed marriages, the temper flare-ups, the strained friendships, the unsatisfying jobs. He came to realize how much he had sabotaged his life as soon as it started to become gratifying because he didn't think he deserved to be happy.

Seeing Yourself Clearly

Now it's your turn to connect the dots. Some upheaval has occurred in your life that has made it difficult for you to cope and to make sense of your world. Perhaps a cherished loved one has died; or a romance, or a dream. Maybe you or someone close to you underwent a major health crisis, or lost a vital career. Maybe you've suffered a divorce or a miscarriage. Perhaps the disappointments and letdowns in life have simply mounted and you've lost all hope in your faith or in your future. Or maybe you just want to find inner peace because you never felt inner peace before, not really, not for any length of time. If you are suffering right now, if you are scared, angry, hurt, grieving a loss, or simply disillusioned by life's letdowns and unmet longings, you are viewing your world through eyes that have been trained to see *some* things but not *other* things.

It is time now to begin seeing those other things.

The "awakening" begins when you see yourself more clearly. The hero's journey is always a journey forward to self-awareness. You cannot find peace *without* until you find peace *within*.

Who You Are, Have Been, and Can Become

To cope best with loss, you must expand your self-awareness, not limit it. The journey to self-awareness is, by necessity, a journey from the known to the unknown. And the unknown is something many prefer to avoid.

When I ask my clients why they thought, felt, acted, or reacted the way they did regarding a particular troubling situation, the most common response is "I don't know why." This is usually a knee-jerk response to avoid looking for answers that may make them uncomfortable.

As you journey down the Four Paths of Transformation, the fewer insights you have about yourself, the greater obstacles you will meet. And if you repeatedly face these same obstacles in your quest for inner peace, it means that you have become blind to some important aspect of yourself.

- If you are an excessively prideful person and try at all costs to avoid appearing weak, you will resist the Path of Acceptance, which is the very path most necessary for you to walk.
- If you insist that the world should operate according to *your* logic, morality, and order, you will resist any guidance you receive on the Path of Inspiration not conforming to your standards.
- If you insist on knowing ahead of time where all roads lead, you will stumble on the Path of Release.
- If you find it hard to forgive yourself or others, you will fruitlessly labor along the Path of Compassion.

The Authentic You

No matter how much you learn about yourself now, some struggle along each path is inevitable—and necessary. For it is in your struggle that you finally become aware of what long-held attitudes and patterns of responding are no longer helpful and need to be reworked or released. It is in facing life's most arduous challenges that we discover more of ourselves.

The most common regret people have as they near the end of their time on earth is a failure to have lived their most authentic life. Their fears and their inability to recognize their full potential caused them to live a life less fulfilling, less true. As you read this sentence, millions of cells in your body are dying. In the past seven years each and every cell of your body has died and been replaced. And yet "you" still exist. So, who are "you," really? There is no better time to discover the real you than on this journey from pain to peace. You may not think of yourself as a hero, but the hero's journey is not about overcoming all obstacles with superhuman strengths. It is about your struggle to discover more of who you really are in the face of difficulties and challenges.

Understanding Your Reactions

A simple way to greater self-awareness is to more closely examine who you are now, who you have been until now, and who you can become. If you're suffering from heartbreak, you may be reacting in ways quite different than expected. In order to cope better along your journey, it's important to better understand why you are thinking, feeling, and acting the way you currently are. But it is also important to have insight into how and why you evolved the way you did in the years leading up to now. Why do you have the strengths you possess? The fears and insecurities? Finally, while you are always in a state of "being," you are also in a state of "becoming." There is a "you" waiting to be born. How can you discover that part of yourself?

Following is a series of explanations about feelings you might be having, along with self-reflection exercises. My hope is that even just one of them will give you an insight into yourself that you didn't have before.

Who You Are Now: Understanding Your Current Emotional State

If your life has been recently upended by loss or trauma, there are four primary reactions you may be experiencing. All of these are normal but must eventually be transcended. These four are:

1. Revisiting the event.
2. Avoiding routine activities.
3. Overreacting to triggers.
4. Regretting past actions.

Revisiting the Event

Your brain tries to help you integrate that loss into your psyche, especially when the grief is overwhelming. When the World Trade Center towers fell, it was such a surreal and painful event in the psyche of all Americans that people watched the video over and over because they couldn't fully process that it had actually happened. "It's unbelievable!" you often heard people say that tragic day. Repeated recollections of the event are your brain's way of helping you to understand and accept that it really happened, although for some people it can become an obsession.

The Path of Acceptance is especially helpful in easing and transcending that reaction.

Avoiding Routine Activities

Your brain, trying to cushion the blow of a major loss, helps you to avoid situations that may remind you of the event by dulling your senses and fogging your mind. People who walk around dazed and confused after a sudden tragedy, such as a devastating tornado, or someone who stays in bed day after day after the death of a loved one, are not yet able to fully face what has happened. Their psychological defenses are operating to keep them somewhat dulled to the enormity of the event in order to face the truth in small doses. The problem arises when they refuse to become fully engaged in daily life over too long a period of time.

The Path of Inspiration is especially helpful in easing and transcending that reaction.

Overreacting to Triggers

Your brain regards what happened to you as a threat to your overall health. It then also works to further protect you by making you react quickly should anything else be reminiscent of the original trauma. When my daughter Anna was six years old, she was accidentally hit in the head by a baseball bat swung by a youngster. While, thankfully, she recovered quickly, I found myself reacting with fear even months later anytime she had even a minor cut or injury. My wish to protect her was so strong that I would overreact to anything remotely resembling a threat to her safety. Overreactions correspond to our increased mistrust and fear.

The Path of Release is especially helpful easing and transcending this reaction.

Regretting Past Actions

Your brain sees regret and blame for past actions as a way to keep alive the illusion that if you could have done everything right that first time, you might have been able to prevent the loss or heartbreak. If the fault lies within yourself (rather than with God, the universe, nature, random events, or other people), then by fixing yourself you falsely believe you can prevent future loss. It is a superstitious type of thinking.

The Path of Compassion is especially helpful in easing and transcending this reaction.

Who You Are Now: Understanding Your Emotions in General

There are four broad areas of emotion: sad, mad, bad, and glad.

- Sad includes depression, regret, and pessimism. A serious depression usually involves self-criticism and a sense of hopelessness.
- Mad includes frustration, resentment, and hate.
- Bad includes fear, guilt, and panic.
- Glad, the golden ray of hope, includes contentment, happiness, and love.

Complicated Grief

Those experiencing a loss often face intense grief. Grief is a combination of several emotions, usually sadness and fear, but also often including anger and guilt. When Jim's father passed away at age ninety, Jim felt sad but also grateful for having had his father in his life for so long. His grief was uncomplicated. A complicated grief is one where the survivor may feel intense fear ("I can't imagine being happy without this person!") or guilt ("I should have acted differently while he was alive!") or rage ("How could God allow this to happen!").

Complicated grief can also occur when a cherished loved one dies unexpectedly or tragically. The more complicated your emotional state, the more likely you will express a wide range of feelings that sometimes contradict one another. For example, when Joanne's husband Bill had a brief extramarital affair, she was devastated. She felt frightened at the prospect of losing Bill, frightened at what her future would be without him, but also furious at his betrayal. She fluctuated between blaming him and blaming herself. Initially, she felt afraid to express too much anger at Bill, fearing it would push him further away. Once their relationship was more secure and she was not fearful of losing him, she allowed her anger to come forth. When your emotions are mixed and extreme, it can appear as if you have a dual personality and you can feel out of control. It helps to understand that emotions are often layered and rarely are 100 percent purely one feeling or another.

One Feeling Leads to Another

The late psychiatrist Dr. David Viscott revealed in his book *The Language of Feelings* that painful emotions have hurt or loss at their foundation and they build from there. Fear of future hurt or loss is experienced as anxiety. Resentment over hurt or loss is experienced as anger. If you don't understand or come to terms with your anger, you will do something to either hurt others or hurt yourself and guilt will result. In other words, hurt or loss can build to fear or anger. Anger can build to guilt. Loss, anger, and guilt that are not managed well can build to depression. Embedded within depression is often a fear that things will never get better.

Understanding What Lies Beneath

This question remains: What is the nature of the hurt or loss that leads to all of those other emotions? Frank, a burly man in his thirties, wanted help for his road rage. He was convinced that his fury at other drivers could not be connected to his experience of hurt or loss because the two emotions seemed so different.

"What bothers you the most about other drivers?" I asked.

"I feel they are trying to control me," he said.

I explained to Frank that there are four primary sources of hurt or loss that, when they occur, will cause us to feel sad, mad, or bad.

The four sources of loss are the loss of:

1. Safety
2. Love
3. Confidence
4. Control

After further discussion, Frank realized that his road rage not only represented a loss of control, but a loss of confidence and self-esteem. He took it personally when other drivers cut him off in traffic. It was a blow to his ego.

Maria and her eighteen-year-old daughter were in their car stopped at a red light when another car swerved and hit them head-on. Maria's daughter was killed and Maria suffered all four areas of loss. She no longer felt that the world was safe. She lost a daughter she dearly loved. She lost her role as devoted mother, always a source of confidence and self-esteem. And she felt as if her life had spun out of control.

By identifying how all of your painful emotions build upon hurt and loss, and by understanding which of the four types of loss—safety, love, confidence, and control—affect you the most, you can see more clearly what areas of your life need to improve and heal for you to experience inner peace.

Who You Have Been: Understanding Your Past

There are several simple but key questions that, when answered honestly, can provide you with tremendous insight into yourself. Your upbringing is important because it is there where you learned basic attitudes that became embedded into your nervous system. Did you learn to trust or mistrust others? Did you gain autonomy and competence or dependence and incompetence? Did you explore your world and take initiative? Did you feel guilty? Did you feel a part of the greater community or isolated? Did you ever worry about abandonment or rejection? If so, did you avoid others so as to avoid being rejected? Or did you cling to others?

Key Question #1: What would you have liked to receive (or receive more of) but didn't get from your childhood?

Whatever you think you did not get enough of will cause one of two extremes:

1. You will find yourself once again in a situation that leaves you wanting.
2. You will succeed in getting it but it will never be enough.

Someone who did not get enough attention as a child may find themselves in situations where again they are ignored or taken for granted. Or they may seek and receive a great deal of attention but it is never enough. These represent inner, unmet needs that will reveal themselves under conditions of crisis, transition, or great loss.

Key Question #2: What do you wish people would understand about you that they often don't?

This, too, may harken back to childhood frustrations or losses, although it may reflect more recent concerns. Do you feel taken for granted? Do your feelings get hurt easily? Do you show your love and devotion in ways that others do not always appreciate? Do you have deeper yearnings that others dismiss as naïve or impractical? When you don't feel understood at a heartfelt level, the lonelier you will be and the more arduous your journey through loss will be.

One trait of those who consistently yearn for others to understand them better is to overfunction—to give more than they receive, and then feel victimized. The major mistake they make is presuming that it is the fault of others who refuse to understand them rather than discovering a deeper truth: they also do not fully understand themselves. If they did, they would stop trying to win people over in order to feel loved. Instead, they would try to be the best person they could be and let those who appreciate that remain in their life and those who do not appreciate that be allowed to move on.

Key Question #3: What was your family role in your childhood?

In a healthy family, children are raised to feel safe and loved, learning to grow up and become mature citizens who can give back to society while achieving their own personal goals. Common childhood roles include the protector, the confidant, the rebel, the peacemaker, the scapegoat, the ghost, and the caregiver. Overdone, these roles can lead to a host of insecurities including difficulty trusting others, a feeling of inadequacy, a need to be in control, a need to always be right, inability to set or respect emotional boundaries, and a fear of rejection. These roles can become so engrained that you either continue them in adulthood or try over and over to shed them.

For example, if you were a confidant to a parent (which prematurely elevates the child to adult status), you may more readily become a confidant to others but be less aware when it is best to let people handle their own problems without your involvement. If you had to look after younger siblings because your parents were working or one of them was ill or unavailable, you may take on the role of caregiver automatically in your adult relationships and always put the needs of others ahead of your own. If you hid as a ghost from your family to avoid being hurt, you may develop self-reliance but also grow to mistrust others.

Each role has the potential for a positive and a negative impact on one's life. Generally speaking, the more rigid the role and the less emotional support received, the more the positive and negative aspects will show up in future relationships and be a source of inner conflict.

CHILDHOOD ROLES		
YOUR ROLE	THE POSITIVES	THE NEGATIVES
The Protector	Assumes responsibility	Neglects own needs
The Confidant	Listens and advises	Oversteps boundaries
The Rebel	Stands for fairness	Opposes all authority
The Peacemaker	Cultivates compassion	Blind to manipulators
The Scapegoat	Defends the downtrodden	Feels victimized
The Ghost	Learns self-reliance	Mistrusts intimacy
The Caregiver	Develops generosity	Assumes martyrdom

The more self-aware you are, the better you can make a conscious choice to repeat an old pattern or not, depending upon the appropriateness of the circumstance. Along the journey of transformation, your goal is to enhance the positive aspects of your childhood role and transcend the negative aspects.

Who You Have Been: Understanding Your Blind Spots

The divorced mother of two teenage daughters, Helen wanted to know why she remained too long in unsatisfying relationships. She told me her parents were never warm or affectionate with her when she was a child. Often she would be left with relatives while they went on vacations without her. One day she said, "I love giving and receiving affection from the men I am dating, but I dislike any affection from my children." She felt guilty, realizing she was doing to them what her parents did to her, but she couldn't help it. "When they were babies I had no problem showing them affection. But now that they are older, I think they shouldn't act so needy."

What Is Projection?

The culprit behind Helen's problem was the defense mechanism "projection." Projection is one of the most common defenses and it can wreak havoc in relationships and make it difficult to get past emotional injuries. Projection happens when a person is unable to recognize an unflattering personal quality but sees that quality in others. So a person who keeps important secrets from a spouse may accuse that spouse of being untrustworthy. In Helen's case, she came to realize that never having received affection when she was a child made her crave affection from men. But her need for affection was so strong she would stay in relationships that were problematic just to receive it. On a deeper, subconscious level, she hated that about herself.

She hated her own desperate need for affection but was unaware of that neediness. Instead she projected onto her children that *they* were too needy, and she therefore pulled away from them when they sought affection from her. She made *them* the problem.

Turning Projection on Its Head

In her book *Loving What Is,* Byron Katie offers readers a simple way to uncover their own projections. Write down any negative judgments you have about others or your situation. You might write "God doesn't care about me" or "I can't easily trust others" or "My husband doesn't take my feelings into consideration." The next step is to rearrange the pronouns or rearrange the meaning of the sentence to its opposite.

- The statement "God doesn't care about me" becomes "I don't care about God" and then "God does care about me."

- The statement "I can't easily trust others" becomes "Others can't easily trust me" and then "I can easily trust others."

Then ask yourself this: Do the new, revised sentences have any merit whatsoever? Even a little? If you resent someone not taking your feelings into consideration, are you overlooking ways in which you don't take their feelings—or even your own—into consideration? Any deeper truth you uncover about yourself is best dealt with first—before you focus on what is wrong with others.

Changing Beliefs about Loss

When you suffer staggering, heartbreaking losses, it is not unusual to believe that life is unfair and that hope for a happy future is now dim or completely dark. While those may be temporary attitudes for some, they can linger for years for many others. It can be helpful to take a closer look at those beliefs and then reverse them. "Life is unfair to me" might become "I am unfair to life" or more pointedly "I am unfair to me." When grief takes over, we often fail to see the ways we are unfair to ourselves by limiting our own opportunities for some degree of inner peace.

Katie also suggests that when you make any strong, negative comment about yourself, others, your situation, or your future such as "I'll never be happy again" or "It doesn't pay to be a good person" or "God has let me down," ask yourself the questions "Is that really true?" and "Do I know for sure that's true?" An honest reflection may help you to change those beliefs to something more valid and more helpful.

Who You Have Been: Understanding How You Cope

Think about a memory from your childhood, one in which you felt scared, inadequate, neglected, abused, betrayed, or belittled. Maybe you overheard your parents fighting and it frightened you. Maybe you were bullied in school. Maybe you had to care for your younger siblings and felt frustrated that you had little time to spend with friends. Try to recall as many details as you can about that situation, especially the emotions you felt.

The important overall question is this: How did you deal with that situation? Fundamentally, there are five ways to cope:

1. Fight
2. Flee
3. Freeze
4. Fold
5. Face your fears

When you examine how you deal with current major life problems or losses, you may be surprised to discover that your primary coping method resembles the method you used when you were young.

When she was growing up, Melinda's parents were very strict. Her father, a minister, insisted that his children behave perfectly. He would not tolerate any embarrassment in front of his congregation. Instead of complying, Melinda became a rebellious teenager and promptly incurred the wrath and disdain of her father. Now an adult, she was attending therapy because her husband had asked for a separation. His main complaint was that Melinda was incapable of compromising. It was her way or the highway. Always.

Melinda's method of coping was to "fight." She spent her childhood in a near-constant fight against her father's controlling methods. Now, ironically, she would fight against her husband, being just as controlling with him as her father had been with her.

Each of the five coping methods may be useful and even wise and necessary in some situations. But if it becomes an automatic way of responding to a situation, your old way will no longer serve you.

Fight

Sometimes you need to fight to survive, persevere, or oppose what is wrong or harmful. The negatives of fighting include unnecessary aggression and projecting your own undesired or disowned qualities onto others. This happens every day in the political arena. A politician calls attention to his opponent's "lies" or scandals, while overlooking or justifying his or her own bad behavior. Reflexively blaming or demeaning others while failing to examine your own role in a situation is another aspect of "fighting."

Flee

Sometimes it is smart to run. Steering clear of an angry, reckless driver might save your life. Fleeing can take many other forms, though. It can mean staying in bed, unwilling or unable to get out in the world. It can mean withdrawing from situations that are challenging for fear of failure or thinking you might make the situation worse. Pretense and denial are two defense mechanisms that are a form of fleeing, as you turn a blind eye to truth. People in abusive relationships often pretend that the abuse is not that bad or that it is somehow deserved. Alcoholics often deny that their drinking has gotten out of hand. Any form of addictive behavior is a way to withdraw, a way to flee from one situation and move toward something more appealing, yet problematic.

Freeze

Sometimes a person who freezes under stress may simply be taking time to think things through in order to not act impulsively. But this coping style can degrade into indecisiveness or emotional paralysis. We know how some animals, such as deer or rabbits, will freeze when they feel threatened. It is their way to try to avoid detection by blending in, so as to not call attention to themselves. Some people act in a similar fashion when they feel tongue-tied in a social situation, or when out of shyness they sit in the back of the class rather than join in with others. Confronted by the sudden death of a loved one, many people will fade into the background, unable to make simple day-to-day decisions, relying on others to assist them. This common instinct to "flee" might help you cope in the immediate aftermath of a loss, but it isn't a strategy that will help you move on in the long term.

Fold

Inevitably, we must all surrender to realities we cannot change. If we live long enough, we will almost certainly lose people we love, lose some of our health, or lose some abilities. We are imperfect beings who can accomplish and endure only so much. When we learn to peacefully coexist with the harsh realities of life, we will suffer less and feel more grateful for what we have. But some of our experiences can cause us to fold—to give up or give in too soon. People who feel helpless or dependent or incompetent won't persevere when the going gets rough. Traumatic childhood experiences often become embedded in our nervous system. The feelings you had when you were a child—to helplessly surrender to an overpowering situation, or to blame oneself, or to run—will resurface in later years when you are faced with a similar situation that triggers the old emotions. As adults we have more options and abilities than we had as children. But when our lives are turned upside down by loss or adversity, our immediate reaction may be similar to those older patterns.

Face Fears

At different times in our lives, we have all had to face fears head-on. Still, it is common to hold back and hesitate, to procrastinate, and even to avoid facing some fears altogether. People often prefer to operate within a safety zone of predictability and not take too many risks. I have also met people who seem fearless, who take incredible risks, but even they sometimes have deeper-seated fears that they do not venture near. People who try to gain as much control over their lives as possible do so because they often fear loss of control. People who seek approval fear disapproval. People who cling to others fear abandonment or rejection. People who avoid commitment fear loss of freedom and also fear rejection. Ironically, by not facing our fears we draw them closer. People who fear rejection often push away the very people they wish to keep close. People who fear failure often keep themselves from tackling an important task wholeheartedly for fear their efforts won't be good enough. They would rather stop short of succeeding and come up with an excuse ("I didn't have enough time . . . I had other things I needed to do . . .") than to truly give it their best shot and risk failure.

When your life has been turned upside down by some loss or adversity, you will come face to face with your deeper fears. It's unavoidable. But therein lies your chance to transcend them.

Who You Can Be: Understanding Your Strengths and Weaknesses

First, don't be disheartened by your weaknesses and failings—there are always strengths hidden behind them. If you made a list of what you consider to be your strengths, you will notice that they become weaknesses when stretched too far:

- A generous and giving person can get depleted by lack of sufficient self-care.
- A determined person may become so headstrong that he or she fails to see when it is time to change tactics or direction.
- Spontaneity can be good but recklessness is not.
- A patient person might wait too long and miss an opportunity.
- A sensitive person can be oversensitive.
- Giving an honest opinion is fine, but harshness disguised as honesty is not.
- An assertive person can become aggressive.
- A person who is well-organized is proud to be so, but he or she can slip into being preoccupied with details that slow down progress.

- A responsible person who can get things done can also be overly controlling.
- Having convictions is good, but not at the expense of open-mindedness.
- A cautious person is less likely to be taken advantage of, but more likely to hesitate when opportunity knocks.
- A clever person can become manipulative.
- A forgiving attitude is wonderful, but repeatedly tolerating hurtful behavior in the name of forgiveness is not. (Some people put up with a spouse's abusive behavior or a friend who takes advantage because they think forgiveness is important. You don't want to confuse forgiveness with allowing bad behavior to continue. You can forgive, but set limits.)
- Self-sufficiency is a desirable attribute, but refusing to ask for help when needed can be costly—sometimes even dangerous.

Along this journey to peace, you will probably hear yourself saying such things as *"Why is life so unfair? Why can't I find happiness? Why did this have to happen?"* Those questions conceal your deeper fears—that you may never experience love again, that your grief will never end, that you are worthless, and that your life has no meaning. If you examine those fears, you will discover that at their core, they have hidden strengths. You remember a time in your life when you believed love was worth having even though you knew it would end someday; you believed in your self-worth despite personal flaws and setbacks; and you saw a future filled with meaning even though all parts were still forming and the meaning unclear. Begin now to identify the strengths that lie behind your fears and weaknesses.

You will need those strengths at your disposal as you travel on your journey.

Who You Can Be: Understanding Your Highest Self

Picture in your mind an apple. Now become *aware* that you are thinking of an apple. You have just demonstrated that there is a "you" that exists as a calm observer to your experiences. This calm, more peaceful observer is the "you" I want you to be more in touch with right now. You might at first regard this calm, background observer as a simple byproduct of your mind's ability to think in complex ways. There is a great deal of evidence to suggest that our mind, our consciousness, is not restricted to somewhere inside our brain but is in fact "nonlocal" and not restricted to time and space—and so the calm observer "inside" you may not be inside you at all. Some regard that "inner you" as your spirit.

Whether you believe or not that you exist in spirit form, you do possess a higher self. Your higher self is not preoccupied with your physical needs for food, safety, and comfort. It is not preoccupied with your ego's needs for attention or approval. It is not preoccupied with your need to be in control, to earn the award, to win the race. It is not concerned with how much you weigh, how tall you are, how attractive you are, or how much money is in your bank account. Your higher self does not disregard your lower self's ego needs, but views those needs as self-limiting. People get trapped into believing that the *only* way to happiness, fulfillment, or inner peace is either through immediate gratification of desires or through achievements—succeeding where others have failed or having the most "stuff."

The resulting happiness or peace is always temporary and shallow, and each newly minted thrill fades only to be replaced again and again.

The typical problems within the realm of the "lower self" (the ache of loss, the struggle to make ends meet, the personal insecurities, the judgmental attitudes, the feelings of conditional worth, the loneliness and emptiness, the complicated grief) create misery and fuel anxiety. Those anxieties cannot be resolved once and for all at the lower-self level. It is at that level they are perpetuated and any cures are always temporary. It is from a higher-self perspective that lower-self problems are transcended. The higher self is grateful for what it has, rather than angry for what it does not. It seeks to define the good, not the bad. I'll discuss more about the lower self and higher self in the next chapter. It is crucial to understand those distinctions, since finding peace in your heart depends upon higher-self functioning.

Approaching the First Pathway

Your higher self understands that the first pathway you must travel is the Path of Acceptance. That path helps you to accept the current reality: yourself as you are and your situation as it is. It is the fundamental pathway for finding inner peace. It awaits you now. Together we will take this next step.

CHAPTER 3

The Path of Acceptance

"Peace is the result of retraining
your mind to process life as it is,
rather than as you think it should be."

—DR. WAYNE DYER

—— Finding Peace Together ——

"My friends are always telling me how I should grieve," Angela
says with amazement and a twinge of anger. "It's as if they know
how it should be done and somehow I'm not doing it right.
Everyone is always giving me advice. They mean well but they
just plain drive me crazy. And I've had it. Whenever a friend
pipes up with advice, I don't tell them but I think to myself,
'Don't you understand what you're doing?'"

Angela's son Danny had died two years earlier at the age of
ten. Impulsive, as many children are, Danny would jump on his
bike whenever the urge hit him, sometimes neglecting to wear
his helmet. He loved performing acrobatics, going airborne on

his bike, jumping curbs, rocks, even small bushes. One day he attempted a particularly high jump. He somersaulted with his bike but this time failed to make a safe landing, striking his head on the curb. He lay in a coma for several days before passing away.

"So what advice do *you* have for me?" she asked, almost defiantly.

"For now I'd just like to understand," I replied. "You have enough people offering you advice, many of whom don't really understand what you're going through."

"No one can understand what it's like unless they've been there," she said. After a moment's pause, she continued. "I like hearing his name. So many people are afraid to say his name. I suppose that's because they don't want to remind me that he died. But when I hear his name I'm reminded that he lived. And I like to talk about him. If only people understood that."

"Can you tell me about Danny?" I asked.

Angela began talking to me about her son and all his favorite things: his favorite food, his favorite teacher, his best friend, his love of adventure, and particularly his joy when pulling good-natured pranks.

When she finished she gazed down at the floor. "It should never have happened," she quietly concluded.

Then I gently offered, "I wonder if you are ready to say these words: *I grieve that it happened, and I accept that it happened.*"

Angela closed her eyes, tears streaming down her face.

"I know I have to," she said. "I don't want to accept it, but I know I have to."

The Path of Acceptance was the first path that Angela would follow on her journey to inner peace.

The Acceptance of Reality

When you emotionally accept the "givens" of your situation—even if you hate the things that happened—you tap into a spiritual, universal energy that will move you forward to a deep inner peace. You will discover how events that would have otherwise knocked you down or made you miserable no longer possess power over you. Still, emotional acceptance is the most misunderstood pathway to inner peace and the most resisted. Have you ever spoken or thought these words: *"I can't accept what happened because it is unacceptable"*? If you have, then you do not yet understand what emotional acceptance is and what it is not. Understanding it will be one of the more important insights you will ever learn.

This next exercise, helpful and revealing, will show you how acceptance can transform your pain into peace. It will also show you how you resist acceptance.

Easing Your Tension: A Guided Meditation

What might be troubling you? Maybe your job is in jeopardy or already lost. Maybe your relationship with your spouse or life partner is falling apart. Maybe your bond with your children is strained. Maybe a dear friendship is at the breaking point. Maybe a loved one has passed away, and you miss her terribly every day. Maybe you are facing a serious health crisis. Or maybe you just feel very alone in this vast world. Try this guided meditation to ease some of the tension that your loss—and the resistance to accepting it—has created.

Imagine you are walking alone down a winding road, stretching as far as the eye can see. It is dark and windy and you are far from home.

The road is surrounded by deep woods on one side and a deep valley on the other. At the bottom of the valley, there is a river swirling in the darkness. The wind is gusting and with each gust there are flashes of lightning. You feel lost and frightened. If all this weren't enough, you are troubled by a worry or loss for which you struggle to come to a clear resolution. You don't know what to do but this much you do know: this problem will forever change your life.

Trudging along this rough road, you start to magnify your worries, imagining all manner of negative outcomes. As you do, the tension in your body rises. You then desperately try to push aside the negative thoughts and replace them with positive ones, telling yourself, "My imagination is running wild. I'm sure everything will turn out fine. This will pass." It calms you—for a moment—but it isn't long before the negative thoughts return. You start to feel overwhelmed. "But what if it DOES get worse? How can I know for sure it won't?"

Like a metronome, your thoughts swing back and forth, creating exasperating and exhausting debates in your head. "What if this happens? What if that happens? Maybe it will. Maybe it won't. But what if it does?" As you argue with yourself, you notice the tension concentrating in your head, your throat, your chest, or your stomach.

This road you are on now takes a turn. You round the corner and an unexpected vista opens before you. Down below is the fast-moving river and above it, barely visible in the dark, a bridge. For the first time you feel more hopeful, but you also realize that you are between two worlds. Do you stay where you are or choose the other side? Choosing the world beyond the bridge means leaving the world you know behind. Is there someone over there to help you and guide you? There are hopeful signs but no perfect answers. Finally you arrive at the foot of the bridge, exquisitely crafted of timbered wood. It arches gracefully over the river, and down again to the other side. Something about this bridge beckons you—it is sturdy, serene, and inviting—and you wonder what you will discover if you cross it. Still, you make your first, tentative steps upon the bridge. As you walk, you start to feel lighter. You look down and the dark, swirling river water begins to transform. Eddies of clear water emerge and darkness gives way to sunlight. Your pace quickens. Peering over the edge now, you see yourself mirrored in the glasslike surface of the water. The sunlight warms you, any sense of urgency subsides, and you allow yourself to relax and just "be."

Then as you breathe in, you think of these words: "I accept my problems and worries as they are at this moment. I accept my situation as it is right now." Now exhale. You start to feel relief as you continue with the words: "I accept my life as it is right now." You stand at the center of the bridge and look back from where you have come. Then you turn your gaze to what lies ahead. The place where you were and the place where you are now seem to be two very different realms. Is it magic? No, but it is remarkable. Intrigued, you march onward knowing that this time there may be a real opportunity to experience inner peace.

Now that you have finished, what happened to the tension in your body? For many it diminished, maybe not entirely—not yet—but you noticed that as you repeated the words *"I accept . . . "* you felt more at ease, a little more freed from your burdens. Your breathing also changed. When you were emotionally opposed to your problem, your breathing was tight and restricted. But with acceptance, you inhale and exhale more freely. You feel calmer.

What you just experienced has extraordinary implications for the inner peace you seek and for every other aspect of your life: your relationships, your career, your health, your self-esteem, and your spirituality.

If instead you felt an *increase* in tension when you spoke the words *"I accept my situation as it is at this moment"* then your energy is blocked. It means you either don't yet fully understand the concept of emotional acceptance or you are confined to a level of awareness that limits your ability to find peace. That level of awareness is a kind of limbo, but a better realm waits. That bridge you crossed is the beginning of the Path of Acceptance and it does indeed bridge two distinct realms. The first is your lower self, the one that is fear-based and often influenced by your unconscious mind and your ego's needs for security and control; the second is your higher self, the one that is love-based and influenced by a super-conscious mind and a sense of oneness with others and the world.

Understanding the Path of Acceptance

Acceptance is the willingness to let go of your emotional opposition to the reality of "what is." While acceptance sounds passive, it is not necessarily. It doesn't mean you won't take steps to change what is possible to change. What if you don't, for instance, get hired for the job you desperately want and need? If you emotionally accept that reality, you will still search for other jobs but you will do so with far less drama or angst. Acceptance is saying "Yes" to reality. It doesn't mean "Reality is good" or "Reality is desirable." Acceptance of a situation does not mean that the situation is morally acceptable. It means "It is." Once again, slowly breathe in and out, then say these words: *"I accept the situation as it is right now even if I don't like it."* Breathing in acceptance when the situation is painful is like being inoculated for a disease. It allows you to take in a bit of what ails you to ward off the greater, more deadly disease. When you accept what is, you can then figure out with greater calmness and clarity what, if anything, you might do about your circumstances.

When things are not going your way, and especially when it's impossible for them to go your way because events have already transpired and cannot be changed, can you let go of the idea that things *should* go your way? Some of my clients have flash-fire tempers. They get annoyed easily at traffic jams, long checkout lines, and just about anything that goes wrong.

"It sounds like you are telling me you should never be inconvenienced while driving or shopping," I say to those who are resisting acceptance.

"But I'm in a hurry!" they reply.

"But is it realistic to expect perfectly moving traffic just because you happen to be in a hurry?" I ask.

When you resist reality, you hand over the power of your emotional well-being to that reality—to other people or events. You are basically saying that for you to be happy or at peace, others must act in a particular way at a particular time, other-wise you have the right to be upset. Is that really how you want to relate to the world?

Pain, loss, and injustice are inevitable. They are part of life's givens. To accept these givens is not to sit back helplessly in the face of them. It is always good and desirable to do what you can to ease pain, comfort the grieving, meet challenges, and treat others and ourselves kindly and fairly. Acceptance frees you to use your energy wisely rather than deplete it with unhealthy attitudes and endless questions that only add to your pain.

Anytime you are in emotional pain and begging an answer to the question, *"Why did this have to happen?"* it means there is a bridge in front of you and the Path of Acceptance waits. If you emotionally oppose the Path of Acceptance, you will have no choice but to turn back and walk its counterpart: the Path of Resistance.

The Path of Resistance

Try to say the following statements: "Just for this moment and without judgment I will:

- Let my emotions be as they are.
- Let others in my life be who they are.
- Let my pain be as it is.
- Let my situation be as it is.
- Let reality be what it is."

Did you have difficulty doing that? Did you hear yourself saying "No!" or "I can't!"? If so, that indicates resistance. Resistance is common, but it prolongs suffering. Anytime you resist the reality of what is, you will have no choice but to suffer more. Resistance comes down to two fundamental emotional drives: fear and desire. Grief is a special combination of those two. You fear your life may never be happy or meaningful after suffering a profound loss, and you desire relief from your pain and a return to a time before the loss. When you are grieving, fearing the future, or desiring something you treasure but cannot have, it isn't easy to say "I accept what is" and mean it. But it is possible and, most important, it is necessary.

Fear and desire are natural. Fear protects you from harm. Desire motivates you to succeed and accomplish wonderful things. When you need to accept a situation you don't like, fear of the unknown and desire to return to the way things were before calamity struck foster emotional resistance and block inner peace.

Fear and desire are the human aspects of your lower self that, given the choice, prefers control to growth or love. Your lower self is at times motivated both by unconscious desires and from beliefs that limit personal growth. Examples of such beliefs are those that justify bad behavior for selfish reasons, or those that cause a person to flee from challenges rather than face them. Some of your fears and desires are instinctive; others are learned. Instinctively, we all possess a fight-flight response when faced with a threat. Sometimes, however, our vivid imaginations create a fight-flight response to circumstances that are not really threatening. You are not born with fear of making a mistake. And there are some things we instinctively need and desire—food when hungry, warmth when cold, and sex when aroused. Other desires are not biological but stem from the need to feel accomplished or productive.

The Limits of Your Lower Self

Thankfully, your lower self is rarely that destructive. You often need what the lower self offers. It represents a way of thinking and navigating the world that helps you to protect yourself, learn skills, and achieve. It is essential that you do not try to completely quell your lower self. It will only go underground and work against you in your unconscious mind. There is a better way.

In his book, *Healing the Culture,* philosopher Robert Spitzer wisely points out that the better way is realized when one's basic needs for safety, comfort, self-esteem, and companionship are used for a greater, more noble purpose. The level of fulfillment that results is enduring and deep. Your lower self's need to achieve—if managed by higher-self values—can instead propel you to use your accomplishment for a greater good. Your lower self's need to fight or flee when responding to an act of betrayal might instead be counteracted by a desire to understand and forgive if higher-self values are allowed to operate.

When you have a soul-stirring experience upon hearing a soaring piece of music, or seeing a stunning view of nature, or witnessing the birth of a child, or holding close a cherished loved one, you are in the presence of your higher self. Your lower self seeks gratification of physical needs or affirmation of worth by acquiring material things or achieving certain ego-gratifying goals. Your higher self doesn't denigrate basic needs or wants, but affirms innate human dignity regardless of accomplishments or possessions. The higher self—what some might refer to as one's soul—affirms a person's worth by simply being connected to God or to an eternal, universal Source. The higher self views everyone as being intimately connected to all others and all things. Therefore, whatever you do to and for another, you do to and for yourself.

If you wish to find peace in your heart, you must have greater access to your higher self. To gain that access, you must first walk the Path of Acceptance. The problem for many people is that their lower self is what drives much of their everyday thoughts and actions while their higher self makes brief appearances. The lower self is more ego-based than love-based and cultivates emotional resistance instead of acceptance. It is about wanting more, and the fear of not getting; fighting against, and the fear of not winning; running from, and the fear of being annihilated. Paradoxically, while trying to protect you from harm, the lower self thrives on inner conflict and confusion, adding to your anxiety. The lower self forces endless inner debates and asks questions that cannot be answered with any certainty. *"I feel so angry and yet . . . I feel so guilty and yet . . . I know I should get up and do something but . . . Am I right to feel the way I do? Was it my fault it happened? Could I have done something to prevent it? Can I ever be happy again? Do I have what it takes to move forward?"*

All of your more painful and stressful emotions exist at the lower-self level of limited awareness: shame, despair, anger, hate, jealousy, guilt, anxiety, and fear. Positive emotions such as pleasure and excitement, while enjoyable, are usually temporary because they rely on comfort or achievements that are never constant. You can satisfy your hunger by eating but you will be hungry again later. You can satisfy your need to feel successful through achievement but you will yearn for greater achievements later. That is why those *only* seeking pleasure as a pathway to deep peace or happiness never rest easily. That is why those *only* avoiding fearful situations as a way to stay safe and comfortable must be constantly vigilant. Basic needs for safety, comfort, or achievement—while necessary and part of our human condition—fail to sustain us psychologically or spiritually.

At the higher realms of self, we experience the more powerful emotional states of compassion, love, joy, forgiveness, gratitude, and peace that are deep and enduring. At a higher realm of awareness, you can still dearly love a person who is no longer with you because true love endures. True love transcends the physical. It transcends the ego. It even transcends time and space. Intellectually you understand that the concept "eternal" means "to go on forever." The concept that our universe extends out in all directions—*forever!*—can be mind-boggling. And yet, when you think of someone you love with all your heart, the concept of loving them forever is comforting and not mind-boggling at all.

Bridging the Lower and Higher Realms of Self

You gain access to the higher realms of self by taking that first step on the Pathway of Acceptance. Acceptance is the foundational pathway that leads you away from resistance and toward inner peace. The problems of grief, fear, failure, and unmet desire cannot be permanently resolved at the lower realms of self. Even if you fear loss of health, for example, your body will eventually break down no matter how well you care for yourself. Desire can never be entirely sated, since you always desire something more than what you have. But neither does the higher realm of self "solve" grief, fear, or desire. It helps you to transcend them and integrate them into your being where they can be viewed from a different, higher perspective.

Harry, a seventy-year-old man, lost his beloved wife of four decades, Emily, to cancer. Until she was hospitalized, they never spent one night apart. Her death left him bereft. Sometime later he reunited with his high school sweetheart, Margie. They married and today he is quite happy. Did his new marriage "solve" his grief? No. Emily was irreplaceable. He thinks of her every day. But he eventually transcended his grief. He would always cherish his life with Emily, trusting that they would one day be together, and yet was grateful for his new life with Margie. Those higher levels of awareness made it possible for him to appreciate the beauty of his life, the wonder of true love, the comfort of companionship, and the peace that comes from believing his life has been worthwhile despite loss.

How did Harry get from grief, fear, and desire to gratitude and peace? He crossed a bridge from the lower self to the higher self, the bridge that begins the Path of Acceptance.

The Hidden Power of Acceptance

Accepting your current reality can offer benefits beyond simply avoiding resistance. Take Regina's experience, for example.

Regina came to see me because her panic attacks were limiting her life. Happily married, she lived next door to her elderly parents and gave them assistance when needed. But her panic attacks sometimes prevented her from taking them shopping or to medical appointments. Despite her willingness to assist them, her relationship with her parents had been strained for many years. She had a poor relationship, in particular, with her father, speaking to her dad only when necessary. Regina's father was a recovering alcoholic. An only child, Regina had mostly unhappy memories of her childhood. She remembered that most nights her father would come home late and drunk, stumbling over the furniture, causing china to clatter and break on the floor, and yelling obscenities. Many nights she heard him vomiting as she cowered at the top of the stairs, fearful for his safety and her own. Her mother acted helpless, never thinking to comfort or protect her daughter. Regina always felt so alone and vulnerable.

"He has never apologized," Regina said. "Neither has my mother. In fact, they think that I should get over it. They constantly tell me, 'It happened long ago. Move on.'"

"You barely speak to your father," I said. "What do you hope that will accomplish?"

"Maybe he will understand how he hurt me and finally care enough to apologize and show remorse." Tears ran down her face.

"You want him to see the error of his ways," I said. "I wonder if your panic attacks serve the same purpose. Do you think that if you keep having panic attacks your parents will finally get the message about how much they've hurt you?"

She gave me a look of both puzzlement and recognition. "I never . . . thought of it that way . . . " she said.

"I wonder, if you finally accept the fact that you have never received the love and care from your parents you wanted and needed, would your panic attacks go away?"

Behind Regina's hurt and anger were grief, fear, and desire. She grieved for her lost childhood, she feared her parents would never apologize for the pain they caused her, and she desired that one day they would open their hearts to her and she could finally have the kind of relationship with them she always wanted. Those fears and yearnings kept her mired in hurt and anger. Her first step was to emotionally accept the givens of her life, including the reality that her parents may never be able, with honesty and compassion, to admit their mistakes. If she could give up her quest to receive the kind of love and understanding from her parents that they were apparently unable or unwilling to give, she could be released from her pain.

"You will still feel some sadness," I told her. "You've tried to avoid the reality of that sadness by fighting against what has happened, by trying to force your parents to open their eyes and admit their mistakes. That fight is over. Ironically, by accepting the realities of your life you may get along better with your parents in their final years."

Acceptance gets your mind to stop the storytelling and the judging; to let go of unmet and unrealistic expectations; to stop asking questions that can never be satisfyingly answered. Emotional acceptance also allows for self-acceptance. Self-acceptance is a type of compassion that is directed toward yourself. Deep down, Regina did not accept herself. She viewed the inability of her parents to care for her as evidence that she was unworthy or unlovable. She tried to convince herself—and them—of her worth by helping them day to day, but that only left her resentful of them and just as doubtful of her own worth. You cannot fix or heal lower-self problems of loss and fear using lower-self strategies. It would be like trying to renovate your home by doing nothing more than rearranging the furniture. Until she moved along the path to her higher self—which begins with acceptance—she would always be in pain.

You can experience acceptance without love, but you can't experience love without acceptance. You can experience acceptance without gratitude, trust, forgiveness, or deep peace but you can't experience those qualities without acceptance.

When your life is upended by loss, tragedy, or painful trials, your tendency will be first to travel the lower-self roads of bitterness or fear. Those are familiar roads but cannot lead you where you need to go. The Four Paths of Transformation begin at the foot of the bridge of acceptance and beyond—off the beaten track, outside of your comfort zone, outside of what you call home. But as you will discover, the Paths of Transformation take you to a place of peace that is your true home.

The Acceptance of Joyful Humility

Everything in the universe, from a subatomic particle to the largest star, contains energy. Every emotion you express carries its own level of energy. The emotion of anger feels different from sadness. Contentment feels different from joy.

One of the most powerful and overlooked sources of emotional energy is genuine humility. A humble heart embraces emotional acceptance, and acceptance nurtures a humble heart. Humility is a misunderstood quality. As with acceptance, there is resistance to it by people who view having control as vital to their psychological survival. The need for control is not inherently bad, but it is an expression of the lower self, fueled by both fear and desire. It serves a useful purpose, but only to a point. When control becomes an end in itself rather than a means to a higher end, it leads only to misery. The more humble you are, the less you need. You don't need to control others or to seek validation from them to prove your worth. You don't need to win. You don't need to manage the impressions others have of you. Think of all that emotional energy required to maintain appearances, to fight for the next trophy, to insist that your life should proceed in a certain way and people should act toward you in a certain way.

Humble, you will not be easily let down by others because you nurture the view that all of us fall short at times. Humble, the more joy you will find in the simplest things. Less humble, the more you will judge, blame, compare, compete, feel entitled— and see things not as they are but as you need them to be. You know you are not being humble when you are not feeling acceptance or some amount of joy.

Control Your Own Happiness

In his book *Power vs. Force*, Dr. David Hawkins explains that with acceptance comes a major shift in one's understanding of the world. In a nonaccepting mode of thinking, your happiness depends on events "out there" unfolding in a manner that you require. That makes "out there" your adversary when the outcome is not what you want. You will feel like a victim, helpless, not like the creator of your own happiness. Once you can accept life's givens and the current circumstances of your life, you learn that true happiness and true inner peace rest within you, regardless of what happens outside of you. By accepting a given reality, you sidestep judgments about right or wrong and instead look at the picture as a whole so you can figure out how best to proceed. You are not only on the receiving end of what life hands you, you are also on the giving end. And *what you do, not what others do to you,* ultimately determines your soul's growth—or shall we say, it determines the growth of your higher self.

Humble people don't stop seeing the true value of themselves, and they never stop seeing the true value of others. When you approach life humbly, you are open to learning. Less than humble, you close yourself off to views or people that don't fit with your ego's need for certainty, to feel right, safe, or superior.

Humility and the Lower Self

Humility allows for possibilities that our ego refuses to acknowledge. In a humble state of mind, you remove your blinders, seeing things as they are instead of the way your ego needs them to be. In J.R.R. Tolkien's timeless saga, *The Lord of the Rings*, the wizard Gandalf holds back the hand of young Frodo, who wishes to end the life of the menacing creature Gollum. Gandalf wisely advises Frodo that one can never foresee all ends and that even the things we despise may later play a role in our redemption. Unhindered by lower-self fears, there is honesty in humility. If you wish to know a deeper truth, be open to hearing more answers even if the information you already have supports what you want to hear.

With emotional acceptance and the energy of humility, you can coexist peacefully with opposite attitudes with which you would otherwise battle: wanting answers but knowing they may never come; loving another but not always feeling loved; risking but wanting to be safe; having convictions but being open to a greater truth; seeking togetherness but needing space; surrendering but possessing some control. Acceptance is inclusive and tolerates uncertainty. Resistance is exclusive, intolerant of uncertainty.

Don't Judge Too Quickly

In order to cultivate emotional acceptance and reduce emotional resistance, notice how often and how quickly you judge others or situations. Having standards of right and wrong is not the problem. Setting boundaries is not the problem. But when you impulsively judge others, there is usually something about them, and yourself, that you do not understand. If you desire to be less judgmental, begin with acceptance. Simply say "Yes" to what happens and try to understand it before you set out judging it or trying to change it. People are often surprised at how often their first reaction to a person, an event, a thought, or a feeling is a resounding "No." You can see how easy it is to emotionally resist the reality of the moment, fail to understand something, and thereby create unnecessary angst.

Do you take things too personally? Are you easily insulted or disappointed by others? Those reactions stem from your ego, which has its basis in fear and desire. It might sadden you if someone you care about overlooks you, disappoints you, isn't there when you need them, or rejects you. But what others might say or do to you often says much more about them than about you.

Lessons Learned?

The struggle to figure out the deeper reasons why bad things happen will keep you spinning your wheels and prevents emotional acceptance. It has been said that bad things in life happen so that we can learn lessons. My problem with that explanation is the implied causality: *because* there is a lesson we have yet to learn, something bad will happen so that we may learn it. I could never imagine saying to a grieving parent who lost a young child in a tragic accident that their child died so that lessons could be learned. I do believe we are on earth to learn and grow. And I know from my experience as a psychologist that some of our hardest but most important lessons are learned through loss and suffering.

Wisdom and perspective are rarely achieved sitting in a rocking chair contemplating the meaning of life. They are achieved by pain born of love: when we sacrifice for the good of others; when we lose something precious and still feel grateful; when we comfort those in pain even when we need comforting.

But the fact that we can grow and learn despite adversity does not mean that the adversity happened precisely for that reason. My philosophy is not "Bad things happen *because* we need to grow." My philosophy is this: "Bad things happen. Accept that and grow anyway."

The Next Path

When you emotionally accept the things you cannot change, you will notice that much of your fearful mind-chatter subsides, such as the endless questions that can never be answered, the regrets, and the yearning to go back in time and change what happened. Then you start a journey that leads to peace. Remember, you cannot halt your journey. It is an inevitable consequence of life's hardships and heartbreaks. You may stumble and fall and feel completely lost at times, but your journey will continue.

The only choices you have are which paths to follow when you encounter them along the road. By choosing the Path of Acceptance you avoided the Path of Resistance this time around. But the Path of Resistance runs parallel to each and every path you take and you will be tempted to cross over to it again and again. Anytime you say "No" to any necessary aspect of your journey, you have wandered onto the Path of Resistance.

It is common to feel completely lost on your journey, to be unsure of where you want to go, let alone how to get there. Up ahead lies the Path of Inspiration. Walk with me along that path and your eyes will be opened to possibilities you may not have considered until now. You will discover that the invisible world will influence your sense of peace more than the visible world does. Avoid this path and you will run into its counterpart: the Path of Illusion.

Let me be your guide along the Path of Inspiration, the next step in your journey.

CHAPTER 4

The Path of Inspiration

"Faith is the bird that feels the light
when the dawn is still dark."

—RABINDRANATH TAGORE

—— Finding Peace Together ——

Sleep was impossible, even though Debra and Mark had been awake for most of the past forty-eight hours. Now it was almost midnight, New Year's Eve. While the rest of the world was getting ready to pop open a bottle of champagne to celebrate the New Year, Debra and Mark could only wonder how much longer they had to celebrate the life of their newborn daughter, Raegan.

"It's doubtful she'll survive," their doctor told them, grim-faced, a few hours after her birth. These blunt words came from a man the young couple regarded as kind and gentle, a man whose words seemed as painful for him to say as they were for them to hear. "And if she does survive," he continued, "she will never be more than an infant."

Raegan was born with a severe and rare brain malformation that left her with a small head and minimal vision. As long as she lived there would many ongoing medical complications, surgeries, and challenges, but the more realistic expectation was that she would survive for only two weeks.

As the couple slept fitfully that night in the hospital, they were awakened by the sound of their daughter crying. A nurse brought the baby to the bedside and told her parents that Raegan had pulled out the feeding tube and was now, surprisingly, drinking from a bottle on her own. "But she won't stop crying," the nurse said. "Want to give it a try?" Debra held Raegan in her arms and as Mark came to the side of the bed, the baby quieted down and continued feeding. Tears streamed down Deb's face. *It's going to be okay,* she told herself.

Raegan held her own for the next three years, despite her severe mental and physical trials. Then suddenly problems occurred. Raegan was unable to keep food down, choking when she tried to swallow. She ultimately received a feeding tube to try to save her life but the surgery resulted in severe complications: a twisted stomach, seizures, and improperly prescribed medications. There was no doubt now among the medical professionals: Raegan really was dying. Debra begged for more tests to be conducted, believing that the doctors had missed something vital. The doctors, more clinical in tone and less sympathetic, told Debra her wishful thinking was not helping matters.

But a couple of days later something inexplicable—some might say "mystical"—happened. Out of the blue, these words popped into Debra's mind: *"It's growing—in my throat, Mommy."* It was as if Raegan was speaking to her telepathically. Debra pestered the doctors who finally gave Raegan a barium swallow study to evaluate her digestive tract. The shocking results left the doctors speechless. "We haven't seen anything like this in twenty-five years," the lead surgeon said. Basically, due to a surgical error, a suture in Raegan's throat had been left in place and scar tissue had formed around it, effectively making it impossible for Raegan to swallow.

Raegan is now fourteen years old. She is legally blind, suffers seizures, cannot speak except for a few sounds, and requires a gastric tube for feeding. "We embrace all of our experiences," Debra told me. "The good, bad, and every place in between. And we've found a beautiful, creative place of family devotion and wisdom through experience." Debra went on to write an award-winning book, *Intuitive Parenting: Listening to the Wisdom of Your Heart,* and start the HeartGlow Center to offer assistance to parents of children with special needs, with the hope of opening a retreat center one day.

Was Raegan somehow able to telepathically communicate to her mother and, by doing so, save her own life? Was Debra's imagination simply joining forces with a lucky guess? Debra believed something more was going on behind the scenes of their lives, something mystical. Having already begun their journey, she and her husband chose to walk together along the Path of Inspiration to see what they would further discover.

Understanding the Path of Inspiration

When you suffer an agonizing loss or misfortune, you undertake a journey you never asked to undertake, and you probably do so with shattered assumptions about your life, the world, and the meaning of life. Your previous ideas of what is right and fair no longer fit this strange new world in which you find yourself. Your expectations have been crushed. In the Biblical tradition, even Christ on the cross cried out, "My God, my God, why have you forsaken me?"

The Path of Acceptance showed you that obsessively trying to understand the deepest reasons why a loss happened would lead you ultimately to frustration and despair. While there may be practical explanations—a fatal car accident occurred due to excessive speed, a spouse had an affair due to marital unhappiness—those explanations don't answer the questions your heart yearns to resolve. The Path of Inspiration leads you to a different understanding—a greater one. This path, when followed with humility and curiosity, leads you toward more important truths about the unseen world and the nature of your existence.

It is a path of faith—the faith that something greater than you can and will, in some mysterious way, support you on your journey.

Guidance along Your Path

This path allows you to grow—not in knowledge, but in wisdom. Your journey is ultimately a quest: to overcome fear, instill peace and healing, and acquire wisdom about the meaning of life. On that difficult road, you will meet a wise teacher who offers inspiration and guidance and who inspires faith. That teacher can take many forms—a holy person, a guru, an elder, God, or even your own inner voice finally awakening to some deeper truth.

The guidance is often couched in language that is imprecise or that raises as many questions as it answers. Throughout history, many seekers of truth have been told by wise counselors that the answers they pursue can only be found "within"—advice that may well be true, yet keeps seekers searching for a more definitive answer. Zen masters use *koans* as a method to break through a young monk's habitual ways of thinking so he may discover a greater truth. A koan cannot be answered with logic. An example of a koan is "What was your original face before you were born?"

Where Does Guidance Come From?

When any of us seek inspiration or answers to profound questions, we might reflect upon nature or read books and poems. Nature speaks as a chorus would sing, in a symphony of movement, colors, sights, sounds, and textures. Poets speak to us in symbolism and metaphors; storytellers may speak in parables. We must sort through their words to discover a meaningful answer, a deeper truth. But deeper truths are often laced with ambiguity and paradox. *To live, you must die . . . To be exalted, you must be humble . . . To embrace, you must let go.* The Bible is a source of guidance for many. But rather than being clear and straightforward, it has been interpreted in a multitude of different ways. In the Harry Potter books, the wise teacher Dumbledore bequeathed to Harry and each of his two friends a separate gift. The gifts seemed insignificant at the time, but eventually played a crucial role in their survival and the victory of good over evil. Dumbledore foresaw the importance of those humble gifts, but the young wizards had to discover that importance for themselves.

Knowledge may be gained through traditional education. But wisdom, if gained at all, is gained through experience and the trials, the tribulations, and the types of meaning we give to those experiences. *Mystical* wisdom is gained by grace—the seemingly unmerited Divine guidance often taking the form of meaningful coincidences and inspired thoughts. Mystical wisdom comes not from what we see but what we don't see, not from what we know but from what we believe, not from what we are taught but from what we deeply sense. Mystical wisdom awaits you along the Path of Inspiration.

What You Will Seek along the Path of Inspiration

The Path of Inspiration asks that you remove the veil over your eyes and be curious about a world that is not material but spiritual, not temporary but eternal. You will never uncover all of the truths of this new world, but it is the *seeking* that matters most, not what you find.

This path is daunting even to those who believe in God, an afterlife, or a spiritual world, for it asks that you expand the limits of what you believe and know in order to be open to that which you may not believe, may not yet know. The reason is that once you are locked into one way of seeing things, you are closed to other ways that may be just as real as or more real than what you believe.

The Path of Inspiration lies just ahead. But if for some reason you resist or emotionally oppose this path, you have no choice but to walk along its counterpart: the Path of Illusion.

The Path of Illusion

This path is deceptive. At first glance it appears ordinary, real, even welcoming. It looks remarkably like most things you have grown familiar with—all your attitudes and beliefs, and the typical ways this world you have grown accustomed to works. But it is an illusion that blinds you to other realities, other truths, that can't be easily discerned or proven.

Avoiding the Path of Illusion

You walk the Path of Illusion when—out of fear—you resist seeking truths that may upset your current beliefs or you refuse to explore life's most profound mysteries. There is nothing wrong with having a solid belief system. There is nothing wrong with embracing a particular religion, or no religion. There is nothing wrong with stating "I believe this to be true and that to be false." What can be self-limiting is when you are afraid to learn about what is different, to explore that which is a mystery, to be curious about that which may run counter to some of your established beliefs. There are several ways to learn and explore further—to avoid the Path of Illusion:

- If you fully embrace a religion, then go deeper into it. There are always hidden insights you have yet to find.
- If you are not entirely sure about any religion, broaden your search to a more personal faith. Search for one that speaks to your heart as well as your head, even if it goes against dogmas you had once been taught to accept without question.
- If you do not believe in any form of religion or spirituality, nurture a sense of awe in the splendor and the mysteries of our universe; be inquisitive about the nature of consciousness.

Galileo stated accurately that the earth was not the center of the universe. That "blasphemy" placed him under house arrest from the age of seventy until he died at seventy-six. The religious authorities of his day did not seek true knowledge but simply confirmation of what they already deemed to be the truth.

Nobel Prize–winning physicist Niels Bohr said, "There are two kinds of truth—a small truth and a great truth. You can recognize a small truth because its opposite is a falsehood. The opposite of a great truth is another great truth." That quote was based upon his discovery that an electron is a particle and it is also not a particle at all. That finding seemed contradictory. Yet it has been proven true. There are paradoxes within religions, too. Some religions tell us to know God on a more personal level yet also tell us that God is unknowable. You need not automatically reject a belief that seems to contradict your own. Both might be true, or not true, or true at a deeper level of understanding.

The Path of Illusion Fosters a Closed Mind

You walk the Path of Illusion whenever you refuse to question your own biases and perceptions, whenever you identify with a group or organization so fervently that you automatically toe the party line rather than allow yourself to be open to other truths. Believe what you wish to believe. Just don't presume there are no other questions worth exploring. Social psychology teaches us that when we believe something strongly, we tend to ignore evidence to the contrary and seek out information that will confirm what we already believe. That is one reason why prejudice and bigotry persist, why political ideologues demonize those who disagree, and why "love is blind."

You walk the Path of Illusion when you feel threatened by those who simply believe differently than you do. The more anger you express when defending your position, the more completely you have attached your ego to an ideology—and your view of the world is more limited than you realize.

The Path of Illusion can be a great obstacle in coping with a loss. Matt had been in a serious car accident, leaving him in constant, chronic pain. His marriage had ended two years earlier, leaving him alone to deal with what he thought of as the devastation of his life. I asked him if he held any spiritual or religious beliefs, hoping that if he did they at least provided him with some degree of comfort. But he responded like so many who've suffered a great loss—with confusion and derision. "I didn't deserve what happened to me," he said bitterly. "If God exists, he's a cruel God," he added. The Path of Illusion tempts us to think in black-and-white terms, with questions about life becoming simplified and, presumably, easier to comprehend. Causes and effects are right or wrong, good or bad, deserved or undeserved. God exists or God doesn't exist; God is loving and powerful or cruel and limited. But with that type of reasoning, all exploration for deeper truths ends. Deeper truths ultimately bring clarity, but often by first muddying the waters. A diamond will glitter—but only after it is found hidden deep within layers of rock and soil, recognized, unearthed, cut, and polished.

How the Path of Illusion Can Deter You

The Path of Inspiration leads you to faith—to believe in something you do not see and to accept the mystery behind it. It then leads you to other areas of an expanded faith, beyond what you already believe. Why? Because tragedies and loss have a way of severely testing faith, often weakening it at first. Along the Path of Illusion, those doubts lead you toward pessimism and the possible abandonment of faith. Along the Path of Inspiration, those doubts lead you to optimism and the possible expansion of faith.

In the heroic journey, the hero starts off weakened by loss or misfortune, forced to wander through a very different world. The hero struggles as he faces "dragons"—trials, losses, and failures—yet still tries to muster strengths he does not know he has. Once inspired, he views his wandering as an adventure, his suffering as temporary, and his weaknesses as reasons for challenge. If he succeeds, he is transformed. Along the Path of Illusion the opposite happens. The hero believes he is a victim, rather than one who can take some control over his fate. He loses his sense of adventure. He views his suffering as permanent and the attempt to rise above it as useless.

The Path of Illusion, because it is familiar, is easily misinterpreted as the proper path to take. But a more profound faith can be found on the Path of Inspiration.

Remain Open to Signs of Inspiration

If you are open to exploring the larger questions of life and your existence, the Path of Inspiration might make itself known through "signs." People talk of these signs all the time—a reminder of a loved one; a seemingly random occurrence that can be shown to have great meaning. Signs alert you to the possibility that more is going on in the world you can't see. They offer hope that guidance from an unseen source is available and will support you as you cope with loss.

I was prompted many times and in many different ways—some might say unusual ways—to write this book. One of the more startling ones happened a few years ago. I had spotted a moth flying around the light fixture above our dining table. As I tried to capture it with a tissue it flew to the other side of the room in that spastic way moths fly. Suddenly it darted toward me like a bullet, barely missing me as it whizzed by.

"Did you see that?" I asked my wife. The moth once again flew to the opposite side of the room. Then once again it came straight at me as if shot from a cannon.

"It did it again!" I cried. "That's not how moths fly!"

My wife gave me her full attention but thought I was being a bit dramatic. Then one last time the moth flew at me from across the room, zooming toward me in a straight line.

That time I ducked, being somewhat alarmed by this freakish event. Then I looked around. Where did it go?

"Do you see it anywhere?" I asked my wife. Just then I felt a fluttering—inside my head, up against my right eardrum. The moth had entered my ear! I told my wife what happened and though skeptical, she gently probed my ear canal with a pair of tweezers, then gasped when the moth emerged, alive but a bit worse for wear. This incredible event aroused my curiosity and I looked up the symbolism of the moth. I learned that moths are called "night butterflies" and that moths and butterflies carry the same symbolism, that of shedding the safety of your cocoon and awakening toward new life—being transformed. I read this quote: "The moth to the flame is the soul seeking the truths of heaven but going through tribulation first." As a psychologist, I already knew that the Greek word *psi* means "soul" and that the word *psychology* literally translates as "the study of the soul." What I didn't know was that the secondary meaning of *psi* is "butterfly." Then I had a strange thought: What if the moth entered my *ear* because there was some message or Divine guidance I needed to *hear*? I had already begun thinking about the idea of writing a book. It would be a book about how I could help individuals deal with losses and misfortunes in life that cannot be changed. Was this moth a sign that it was time for me to start writing that book? Or was I simply letting my imagination get the better of me?

An answer came several weeks later when something even more remarkable happened. I was in my car, waiting in line at a fast-food drive-through. My daughter worked there during the summer and I had stopped by to surprise her and say hello. As I waited my turn, a mourning dove flew in front of me, hovered inches away from my windshield, and stared at me for several seconds. I stared back, both startled and entranced. Finally, it lowered its head, opened its beak, dropped something small and white on the hood of my car—and flew off. Fascinated, I focused on what appeared to be a torn piece of white paper on my car's hood. The paper began to "flutter" and I realized to my amazement that it was not a piece of paper but a moth. Then the moth flew away.

A dove, a symbol of spirituality, had captured a moth, held it gently in its beak while hovering in front of me for several seconds, and finally offered me its food. Then I remembered how a moth—another spiritual symbol—had flown into my ear weeks before. Those events were far too unusual and too coincidental to be a fluke. Later, when I looked up the symbolism of a mourning dove, I read that the call of the mourning dove represents a song of grief over the loss of a loved one. But the dove itself symbolizes something more optimistic and spiritual; it represents hope, rebirth, and peace after loss. The theme of this book—finding hope, peace, and spiritual transformation after loss—had begun to take shape by virtue of a strange and beautiful set of circumstances.

If you open yourself to Divine guidance and inspiration, you will receive it. It may take many forms, but it always requires receptiveness and acceptance on the part of the receiver.

What Is Mystical Wisdom?

The Path of Inspiration provides the energy of mystical wisdom—wisdom that comes not from what you've been told but from a profound, personal experience of something that is keenly felt and hard to explain. A religious person possesses faith, but a faithful person need not possess religion. But all of the great religions, and all loving people, share something in common. They have at their core some version of the Golden Rule: Do unto others as you would have them do unto you. They also seek truth.

Walking the Path of Inspiration is less about what you find than about your willingness to seek. What are you seeking? An experiential relationship with the Divine; something that takes you from the place of "I believe" to "I know." You are seeking mystical wisdom.

By understanding the four aspects of mystical wisdom, you have the opportunity to make the most of your journey along this path. The four aspects are these:

1. Belief that some Higher Power or Unifying Source exists.
2. Belief that this Source is accessible.
3. Belief that once the Source is accessed, signs of its continued presence will appear.

4. Belief that the Source is mysterious, beyond full comprehension.

Any wisdom you receive is not the final answer. There is always more that is hidden, to be revealed later, and more that will always remain mysterious. But your soul embraces the mysterious unknowable as much as it embraces the transparent known. And, as it is with inquiries into matters vast and almost incomprehensible, the more you know the more you realize how little you know.

The Belief in a Source

Along the Path of Inspiration, it is not necessary to believe in God but it is necessary to seek more love, gratitude, and compassion, for those three qualities are powerful, unifying forces. Whether you believe God exists, do not believe, or are undecided, this path will prompt you to re-examine your beliefs and make them a more meaningful part of your life. When I ask my clients about their belief in God, many say that they believe God exists and perhaps there is an afterlife, too. But some say that their beliefs have no bearing on their daily lives. That is not the faith of which I write. To be meaningful, one's faith must play a role in your life; it must motivate you to contemplate the bigger questions and live a life in accordance with the major principles of that faith.

If you believe in God or a Higher Power, your task on the Path of Inspiration is to deepen that belief by exploring life's mysteries, such as "Why do bad things happen to good people?" and "Is there a higher purpose to loss and suffering?" Such questions compel you to delve more deeply into your faith and in the process become more attuned to the hidden wisdom your faith offers. Don't be surprised if your exploration causes you to question your faith at times. That doesn't mean that the tenets of your faith are necessarily wrong. It is possible to accept that your faith says one thing and that your inner wisdom suggests something else. That is all the more reason to be curious and seek greater understanding even if it causes confusion. It is fine to have doubts or to be confused. But don't allow the doubts to stop your search for greater wisdom. Doubts also keep you honest and hungry for greater truth.

The first aspect of mystical wisdom is belief that some sort of Unifying Source—call it God if you like—exists. Belief in that Source can help you to consider the idea that anytime you draw a conclusion based purely on reasoning or your perception of reality, you are limiting yourself. Suffering through an unexpected or unwanted loss, we all have a tendency to believe that the loss "shouldn't" have happened, or that it was "senseless." Sometimes what appears to be senseless makes sense in some larger scheme. Is there a way to understand even a tiny amount of what seems so obscure? Possibly. The next aspect of mystical wisdom is the belief that the Source—and Divine guidance—is accessible.

The Source *Is* Accessible

Can you really talk to God? And if God talks to you, will you understand the message? In my work as a psychologist, many couples come to me for counseling. Their most common complaint is poor communication. A message gets sent but somehow it is misunderstood, never heard, or heard but never acted upon. Most people don't listen as well as they think they do.

So when it comes to listening to God or even to one's own inner voice—especially when you are frightened or grieving— it is easy to miss the message. Discerning inner guidance is like detecting the subtle ripple caused by a single leaf falling upon a lake. If the water is churned by wind or rain, the ripples of a single fallen leaf are not easy to see. The lake, like your mind, must be placid to detect subtle information. When your mind is filled with anxiety, grief-related despair, or endless anguish, it can be hard to detect that "still, small voice."

I left the gym one Sunday afternoon with the intention of driving to my favorite coffee shop. Remnants of a hurricane still battered the area with a hard rain that pummeled the ground. When I spotted the coffee shop I prepared to move into the left lane and turn but, inexplicably, I remained in the right lane. The feeling I suddenly had was a subtle, gentle *"No."* That was strange, I thought to myself. I still had an opportunity to make the turn but as seconds passed I found myself driving past the coffee shop, at a loss to understand why. Ahead on my right was a bookstore with a coffee shop so I decided to stop there. The rain was now falling in sheets but luckily I had an umbrella. I parked, grabbed the umbrella, reached for the door— and stopped. Another gentle *"No"* filled my mind and body. I waited, perplexed as to what was happening, and after about two more minutes I suddenly felt the time was right to get out of my car. As I started to jog toward the entrance, grateful for my umbrella, I spotted a flash of bright red. I turned around and watched as an elderly man wearing a red shirt slowly emerged from his car. I knew that without an umbrella or coat he would be soaked to the skin by the time he made it to the front door. I raced over to him and offered to share my umbrella. He took my arm as though I was family and we walked together ever so slowly to the entrance. Once inside the store he thanked me. Now I can get my coffee, I thought to myself. *"Yes"* came the gentle thought in my head.

Some might argue that such a story is mere happenstance and proves nothing—quite possibly true. What stands out to me is not that it may or may not have been mystical guidance, but that I listened to and obeyed the gentle *"No"* and was curious enough to go where it might lead me. Had my ego been in charge, the logical, practical part of me, I would have brushed aside the thought of *"No"* and driven straight to the coffee shop. Instead, I put aside my ego and ended up helping an elderly gentleman in need. In the beginning, bypassing the coffee shop made no sense to me. In the end, it made perfect sense.

The Power of Prayer

Prayer is the most common way people try to access and communicate with God. According to physician Larry Dossey, author of *Healing Words: The Power of Prayer and the Practice of Medicine*, prayer is best described as a nonlocal event—infinite in both space and time. When praying, you do not "send out" a message to a God "out there." Outside of space and time there is no "out there." Everything is one. God is everywhere. And messages come in even before they are sent out.

The deeper purpose of prayer may not be to ask for things, but asking is one way to cultivate a relationship with the Source. As impossible as it might be to ever "know" God, experience tells us that we know someone *not* when we study, analyze, or judge that person dispassionately from a distance, but when we participate in a close, meaningful relationship. Faith, for too many people, has crystallized into an impersonal system of rules and obligations. Those on the Path of Inspiration seek faith that takes on a more personal tone, a sense of yearning to connect. The connection happens not when the seeker finds God, but when the seeker recognizes that God is both nowhere to be found and everywhere to be experienced, including within.

How to Access the Source During a Loss

As a seeker who experienced loss, you may discover that the reason for God's apparent absence is more likely your fear of showing up. *What will God require of me?* you ask. Asking that question suggests trepidation, fear that God will ask of you what you do not wish to give. *What will it cost me?* you wonder. But what if you believed that all God or the Source asks is that you become the best you can be, your most authentic self, while trusting that Divine guidance will always be forthcoming? It might be just that simple. In trying to comprehend God's ways, I wonder if we have a tendency to complicate what is simple, and simplify what is complicated.

Prayer Throughout Life

Why you pray—and what you pray for—happens to match stages of personal development. Think of the development of an infant through childhood and from childhood through adulthood. There are seven major stages. These stages also correspond to the seven chakras—energy centers of the body theorized by Eastern philosophies, which represent the following needs that exist throughout our lifetime but develop first as we physically grow and mature. These are needs for:

1. Safety, care, and protection (infant and toddler; the root chakra)
2. Family relationships (young child; the sacral chakra)
3. Relationship with oneself (teenager; the solar plexus chakra)
4. Love outside the family (older teenager, young adult; the heart chakra)
5. Self-expression (independent adult; the throat chakra)
6. Vision of a greater world (adult; the third-eye chakra)
7. Wisdom (older adult; the crown chakra)

One or more of those needs may become compromised at any point in your life and you may pray for assistance. Will you filter those prayers through your fears and desires or through higher-self qualities of love, trust, gratitude, and peace? Will you pray for health, safety, and success? Or will you pray for guidance on how to be more loving, more faithful, and more compassionate? At the lower fear-based levels, your prayers will be heard but any guidance you seek may be distorted by your fears and desperation. Have you ever tried to give advice to someone who is frantic, desperate, or grieving? He or she has a hard time comprehending all you have to say. Praying for the safety of a loved one is an understandable prayer, but one filtered through your fear. That same plea, if filtered through your gratitude for having that loved one in your life and your trust in whatever way events play out, allows for inner peace to take hold and Divine guidance to be discerned.

Meditation and prayer—not only when in need but when you are content—are time-honored ways to experience a connection to a higher power. Quieting your mind takes practice but helps you to distinguish those moments of true guidance from wishful thinking or paralyzing fears.

Look for Signs of a Loved One's Presence

It is commonplace for a grieving person to believe that particular happenings and coincidences are "signs" that a loved one in spirit is saying hello. The familiar smell of a grandfather's pipe tobacco in a room where no one smokes, a precious object found at the perfect moment, a special song playing on the radio just when you are thinking about the person who passed away .... Some signs seem to be nothing more than coincidence or an attempt by the bereaved to force a connection that doesn't exist. And that may be true sometimes. But some signs cannot be so easily dismissed.

Julie came to see me after her beloved grandmother had died. She had spent a dozen glorious summers at her grandmother's home when she was growing up. "Carefree days, filled with love," she told me. Julie had heard that one of my specialties was grief counseling and that I was happy to discuss spiritual or mystical matters with any client. "I want a sign that she is okay," Julie said. "I want to know if she is happy and that she understands that I miss her. How do I look for a sign?" she asked.

I explained that genuine signs happen when you least expect them, but that it's important to be open to receiving them. "However," I said, "you might choose a symbol. It could be a special word or object or event that is not common. If that symbol shows up soon, perhaps that is a sign."

It was chilly and December was upon us. Julie decided that her symbol would be a grasshopper. She hadn't seen any all year. "If I see a grasshopper anytime soon—even if it is just on television—I will take that as a sign from my grandmother that she knows I miss her and she is happy."

A few days later I got a call from Julie and she had an amazing story. It had been an unusually warm day for December and she had been sitting outside on her patio, resting her feet on a small table, absorbed in reading a book. When she glanced up she saw a grasshopper by her feet. Amazed, she called a neighbor over to take a look. He picked up the grasshopper—Julie was a bit skittish with insects—and gently placed it in the nearby grass. The next day Julie was sitting on her patio and it happened again. But this grasshopper, almost three times the size of the first, hopped right up on top of the table. Again she called her neighbor over; he remarked that not only was it unusual for two grasshoppers to show up that time of year, but he found it curious that both grasshoppers had been missing a leg.

"What my friend didn't know was that my grandmother was an amputee. She only had one leg," Julie told me.

The day Julie told me her story I had been working late and it was dark outside when I got into my car for the drive home. My car was parked under a streetlamp and I noticed what I thought was a smudge on the outside top of my windshield. I tried to clear it away with the windshield wipers but it was too high for them to reach. When I got home I discovered it was not a smudge after all but a live grasshopper. I hadn't seen one that year at all and I haven't seen one since. What are the odds?

What Is Synchronicity?

Synchronicity is the term used to describe a coincidence that has deeper meaning. The simple act of thinking about a grasshopper and then seeing one would be a nonmeaningful coincidence. But it was very meaningful to Julie because she had chosen the grasshopper as a sign of her deceased grandmother's continued presence. Synchronicities tell us that there is much more going on behind the scenes of our lives than we imagine.

Once you are open to the idea of meaningful coincidences, they tend to occur with greater frequency. They might take the form of perfect timing, like money arriving precisely at the time it is desperately needed. According to therapist and philosopher David Richo, author of *The Power of Coincidence: How Life Shows Us What We Need to Know*, synchronicity is where the two realms—matter and mind—meet. It is where a material event (seeing a grasshopper) connects with a nonmaterial event (a wish to see a grasshopper)—but in a meaningful way. It could be said that synchronicity is one place where humans and the Divine meet.

Synchronicity and Loss

A common yearning among those grieving the loss of a loved one is to have one last real contact, one last goodbye— a touch, a sound, a sight—something on a physical level. It is a completely understandable yearning. We are physical beings that exist on a physical plane and feel things more profoundly when they involve at least one of our five senses. But we are also spiritual beings, possessing an intuition and a consciousness that appear to be nonlocal and beyond space and time. Many of us have also experienced paranormal, psychic, or synchronistic events that cannot be adequately explained by either the laws of science or the condition of happenstance. Since loved ones in spirit exist in a nonphysical dimension, we can become closer to them not when we stay grounded to the physical senses and the ego's need for certitude, but when we nurture higher-self qualities of love, joy, trust, peace, gratitude, and compassion and our soul's need to embrace the unknown. Simply holding a loving thought about someone who has passed on can ignite a spiritual connection. But without a clear physical confirmation of that spiritual contact, we require faith to embrace it. We become closer to them when we open ourselves to the realities of synchronicity. That may be a method they use to reach out to us.

In 2002, I was sitting with a woman who was in deep grief over the passing of her mother. Sandra had cared for her mother during the last two years of her life and watched her suffering increase from the debilitating effects of bone cancer. Listening to Sandra speak, I was distracted by an image in my mind of a woman affectionately embracing a large pumpkin. It seemed to me an absurd image, totally disconnected from our conversation. I quietly scolded myself to remain focused on Sandra, but the image in my head grew more intense and finally impossible for me to ignore. It was as if I was watching a television show with no ability to change the channel or turn off the set. Finally, I interrupted Sandra and sheepishly asked her, "By any chance was your mother particularly fond of pumpkins?"

Sandra's face, downcast just seconds before, now lit up. "My mother loved pumpkins!" she cried. "She grew them as a child. We had a pumpkin patch in our backyard growing up. She was even out planting pumpkin seeds shortly before she died. How did you *know* that?"

Good question.

Over the following weeks and months, that same phenomenon occurred with growing regularity as I counseled people in my private practice. I rarely spoke of it to them but found ways to indirectly validate what my mind was telling me by asking clients leading questions. Occasionally I would inform a client what was happening if I truly believed he or she would be open to it and that it would be helpful. Since then, I've participated in dozens of workshops to enhance this gift and have demonstrated the phenomenon at national conferences. I've gone from someone who "believes" in the survival of consciousness after death to someone who "knows."

Synchronicity and Faith

I understand that one person's paranormal experience does not prove the legitimacy of that experience. But religious and spiritual experiences are often highly personal, deeply meaningful, sometimes profound and soul-stirring, and not usually repeatable at will. As such, they are difficult to verify in a science laboratory. No doubt we can delude ourselves into thinking that an unusual experience has heavenly origins. But don't dismiss them out of hand. In the history of mankind it seems there have been enough mystical and miraculous events to encourage belief, and enough pain, suffering, and unanswered prayers to encourage disbelief. What's left is faith, and the mystery that pervades it.

I also experienced synchronicity after my mother passed away. I had visited my mother six days before she died in her nursing home, about a two-hour drive from my house. It had been at least two years since she had last recognized me, and that day was no different. She was emaciated and looked so small in her bed. An aide was feeding her ice cream while she drifted into a kind of morphine- and dementia-induced haze.

"It's me," I said, as I greeted her with a kiss. "Paul."

"I'm Fran," my mom said, smiling graciously. That was my mom—polite to everyone, even "strangers."

I spent the next ninety minutes reminiscing with her, telling her about my life, reminding her of her family, hoping that on some level she understood. I knew from her appearance— so drastically different from when I saw her just three weeks earlier—that she would soon move on from this world. When it was time for me to leave I kissed her face, not once or twice but maybe thirty times. I knew it might be the last time I saw her. Mom accepted the kisses with no outward sense of awareness.

A few mornings later as I walked through the parking lot to my office, I spoke in my mind to my father, who had passed away twelve years earlier. "Dad," I said. "Would you send me a sign that mom understood all those kisses?" As I entered my waiting room I noticed that all of the magazines on the large coffee table had been placed in perfect order the night before— the handiwork of one of my associate's clients. Curiously, one magazine lay open and askew smack-dab in the middle. I wondered why the fastidious client would take the time to organize all the magazines but then ruin the effect at the last moment. I picked it up and saw that it was open to a page that advertised porcelain figurines. I stared dumbfounded at the ad—a picture of a puppy kissing its mother's face with the caption "Momma can never get enough kisses."

"Thanks, Dad," I said quietly. Mom understood after all. Three days later she passed away.

Accept That the Source Is Mysterious

There are some questions many take for granted without search-ing for answers. Why are we romantically attracted to some people and not others? Why do we choose one career over another? Why do we enjoy some sports, or no sports? Why is one person interested in music while another cares only about astronomy? Why do some of us like vanilla, others chocolate? The questions could go on forever. A common response to any of these could be "I don't know. That's just the way I am." But when it comes to questions about God or a universal Source, we expect more. We demand that it all make sense. We become easily disillusioned when God lets us down.

Rabbi Rami Shapiro, author of *The Sacred Art of Lovingkindness*, says that all religions need to be humble in their beliefs because the closer one gets to God, the further one gets from certainty. We can't even fully define love. We experience it, we know love when we feel it, but any words to describe it just scratch the surface. Love remains a mystery. Yet once in the realm of a loving relationship, that which is mysterious is somehow more recognizable. A parent, devoted to her child, would willingly and instantly sacrifice her life if it meant her child would survive. There is something profound about that level of love.

In the classic book *Man's Search for Meaning*, Viktor Frankl wrote about his time spent as prisoner in a concentration camp in Nazi-annexed Poland. His parents and pregnant wife were killed and he suffered through tortures and indignities. Food was scarce and prisoners died from malnutrition. And yet the prisoners who chose to share their bits of food survived longer than those who hoarded their food. Frankl wrote that "even the helpless victim of a hopeless situation, facing a fate he cannot change, may rise above himself, may grow beyond himself, and by so doing change himself." Something about love and relationship made all the difference. Mother Teresa, famed for her lifelong devotion to the poor, viewed herself as "a little pencil in the hand of a writing God who is sending a love letter to the world." She accepted the mystery of suffering and simply worked to alleviate it, not critique it.

Many of us have difficulty appreciating mystery as it pertains to God and spirituality. In times of pain and calamity, we want God to rescue us. We want solutions, not clichés about how God works in mysterious ways. When the answers we want are not forthcoming, we often doubt God rather than doubt our limited beliefs about how God should act.

When you embrace mystery rather than reject it, you remain hopeful. When you live in accordance with the statement "I believe even though I do not always understand," you remain hopeful. To the cynics, that is foolishness. To the mystics throughout the centuries, it is an aspect of a deeper faith. To the suffering among us who are pleading to an Almighty God for a miracle, embracing a mysterious God or Source is surrender, a form of emotional acceptance and a hope that their suffering leads ultimately to something greater, something more meaningful.

The next pathway is the Path of Release, which is the path of hope. It is not the hope that all will work out exactly as you wish, although that could happen. It is the hope that what does happen will lead you to a more meaningful life. Its counterpart is the Path of Despair, well-worn but, with help, able to be bypassed.

Your journey continues. Follow me.

CHAPTER 5

The Path of Release

"Should you shield the canyons from the
windstorms, you would never see
the true beauty of their carvings."

—ELISABETH KÜBLER-ROSS

────── Finding Peace Together ──────

I carefully placed the notecard back into the envelope, like I
might place a baby bird back into its nest. The message on the
inside that I just re-read, two simple lines from 1995 written in
careful, small script, befitted the humbleness of the man who
penned them. His final three words impress upon my mind even
now: "Gentle Peace—Martin."

In January 1985, gunfire shattered the morning calm as
Father Lawrence Martin Jenco drove to work. He watched in
horror as men fired automatic weapons wildly into the air, scat-
tering shopkeepers, parents and their children, and others simply going about their business in the "safe" section of the city
of Beirut, Lebanon. Those same men then forced their way into
Father Jenco's car, dragged him out, and shoved him onto the

floor of a waiting vehicle. Father Jenco was serving as director of Catholic Relief Services. The Catholic charity supplied food, clothing, and medicine to the people of Lebanon, a country brutally torn in the 1980s by warring Muslim factions. Taken hostage and held for 565 days, he was one of more than a dozen men kidnapped over an eight-year period who languished in tiny, filthy cells in Lebanon. Their captivity made headlines around the world.

Father Jenco spent day after day in solitary confinement, chained to a radiator. His captors rarely allowed him to bathe or clean himself. They permitted him use of the bathroom only once per day. From time to time they beat him. On occasion they would transport him by truck to other secret locations. Bound tightly with rope, a dirty rag shoved in his mouth, he would be forced inside the truck's wheel well—a hot metal box. He strained to breathe through the exhaust fumes while trying to keep from vomiting, knowing that if he did he would choke to death in that cramped tomb. When he reached his destination he would emerge burnt and bleeding. Ironically, his capture should never have happened. It was an accident, a twist of fate. His captors had mistaken him for someone else.

I met Father Lawrence Martin Jenco in 1995 at a conference on forgiveness held at the University of Wisconsin in Madison, where Father Jenco was the keynote speaker. Sometimes during his speech that day Father Jenco would slur his words, the result of brain damage suffered at the hands of his captors. At the conference, nearly nine years after his release, he radiated love, gentleness, and profound humility. When we first met, instead of shaking my hand he opened his arms wide, smiled broadly, and embraced me warmly as he would an old friend. I was a complete stranger, but to Father Jenco we were all "brothers." He had developed a severe eye infection during his captivity and at times was not permitted to wear his glasses. When his vision became severely impaired, a small misplaced item that had become precious to him—a button torn from the coat he had been wearing the day of his capture, would cause him to become frantic. That button, for reasons he did not understand, had become a source of comfort. Father Jenco's moment of transformation occurred when he finally "in all this madness" screamed at God "You can have the button!" and threw it away. Now he was released. His motto from that point on was "Cling to nothing material" and so he trusted only in God. In his book, *Bound to Forgive*, Father Jenco wrote that he had experienced many moments of anger, hatred, confusion, and despair but ultimately kept his faith in God.

Near the end of his captivity, a man named Sayeed, one of those who had brutalized him, began to respectfully refer to Father Jenco as "Abouna" ("Dear Father"). Blindfolded, never allowed to see the faces of his captors under penalty of death, one day Father Jenco heard Sayeed move close to his face and softly speak these words: "Abouna, do you forgive me?" Overwhelmed by the request, Father Jenco forgave his captors. Despite his doubts about the goodness of humanity—doubts cultivated by the horror of his capture, torture, and deprivation—he came to believe that it was better to release doubt and ultimately to trust. There was more to admire in mankind than to despise.

"Gentle peace" was Father Jenco's call sign and his heartfelt prayer for humanity. This good man died, sixty-one years old, of pancreatic and lung cancer the year after I met him and almost ten years to the day after he had been released by his kidnappers.

I could have written of Father Jenco's story to illustrate any of the Paths of Transformation—Acceptance, Inspiration, Release, and Compassion. His story exemplifies the hero's journey. I chose the Path of Release because ultimately he was, literally and figuratively, released. Even he, a man of great faith, stumbled and fell along that path in his moments of despair. Those moments are natural, almost a given, for none of us is superhuman. Still, it is along the Path of Release that we let go of the obstacles to our transformation—our fears, our illusions and irrational beliefs, our need for safety and certainty, our anger at injustice—but only after great struggle.

Understanding the Path of Release

When you earlier walked the Path of Acceptance, you stopped resisting the reality of what "is" and opened a door to a deeper reality. Walking the Path of Inspiration, you experienced a Source that connects you to all living things and assists you on your journey. But the rocky road ahead remains even more challenging. When pain, grief, and fear stop you hard, it is difficult to sustain faith that seems so distant, inaccessible, and illusory. The Path of Release is a path of trust—trust that your faith in a Source will stand despite doubt; trust that your faith in a purposeful future is sustainable despite despair.

The medieval mystic Meister Eckhart said that spiritual growth and transformation come about not from a process of addition but from subtraction. A child emerging from the womb experiences a new world by leaving the old world. The Path of Release is so named because it involves the letting go of false beliefs, of patterns of behavior that limit you, of the ego's needs for control, of your fear of change and transformation. All that is left is to surrender to trust. Trust is what remains when you willingly and peacefully surrender to an unknown future with an uncertain outcome that can perhaps be influenced by you but not controlled by you.

The Path of Release may require the most effort. Just when your journey becomes the most wearisome, your challenges become the most burdensome. This is the part of your journey when the reality of what has happened to you is no longer clouded by shock or denial. You no longer bargain with unseen forces to help you escape or to turn back the clock. You have moved from *"This can't be happening!"* to *"It has happened,"* and the reality seeps into your soul like a bitter winter wind. This is the path on which you must battle the dragons that live in your heart and head. This is the path on which you catch your breath and think the worst is over, only to be knocked down yet again by some other misfortune. This path is paved with ironies and contradictions. You are alone, but you are not alone. The battles fought, the challenges faced are only yours. In the cold, dark night, all you want is to wrap yourself in a warm blanket by the blaze of a fire and dream of better times. But instead you are naked and shivering, and it is ever darker. You call for help but hear only the lonely echo of your own voice. If there is anyone out there—friends, family, a kind stranger, God—no one answers. Yet in this solitude, this desolation, you have no choice but to draw into yourself and ask the big questions: *"Who am I? Why am I here? Where am I going?"*

It is in this spectacular moment, as your outer world begins to darken, that your inner world begins to glow.

The Four Assurances

In times of loss and uncertainty, we hold fast to familiar ways of thinking and behaving that provide us with some semblance of security and predictability. These become our guideposts along a rough road. We hold hands with those we love; we take comfort in traditions; we trust that the night sky will reveal the North Star. But the hardships and losses that break our hearts also fracture our beliefs and rituals, our view of ourselves and others, our opinions of how things should be. Nothing makes sense anymore. We know that death is part of life, that losses are inevitable, but experienced full force we can't believe it's really happening. Those givens of life seem so cruel.

There is a moment in life when we learn that our parents can no longer protect us nor propel us forward. We are on our own. It is then that we grow, achieving a rite of passage—with a sense of excitement, but also with uncertainty. On the Path of Release, the transition is not as simple. Instead, the losses are often gut-wrenching and the life changes profound. It is the difference between growth and transformation. A flower grows; an exploding star transforms.

It is on the Path of Release that you might believe God is with you but you don't feel his presence. You might know that your friends care, but they have their own families to care for and their own homes to go to at night. You might stay busy to distract yourself from your pain, but busywork eventually becomes an empty activity. You may often eat on the run, but when you finally sit down at a table for a proper meal, you notice a dinner plate missing. You then know that your life has been altered forever and that you have descended into a different world. Nothing is absolute and predictable anymore. You exist in a state of limbo. Ultimately, you are forced to release fears and habits that had kept you imbalanced, that did not allow other facets of your truer and fuller self to emerge, so that this truer self can be called upon when needed. In this process of rebalancing, you feel temporarily off-balance, like an observer to your own life, detached and ungrounded. Things may look the same but no longer feel the same. *"Who am I?"* you ask.

Fortunately, there exist four assurances that you may trust as you walk along the Path of Release:

1. You will be compelled—by virtue of your own unique journey—to change your way of thinking.
2. You will receive guidance and insights only after—not before—you grapple with inner conflicts.
3. You will not despair if you learn to peacefully coexist with uncertainty.
4. You will always have the choice to view your life as worthwhile, no matter the circumstances.

The First Assurance: You Will Live Yourself Into a New Way of Thinking

Richard Rohr, Franciscan priest and author of the book *The Naked Now*, says of transformation, "You do not think yourself into a new way of living as much as you live yourself into a new way of thinking"—a statement that is never more true than on the Path of Release. It is there, both in your struggle and your steadfastness, your giving up and your rising up, that you reconfigure the values, attitudes, and philosophies no longer serving you or release them entirely. When faced with profound loss, you will inevitably struggle to regain control over your life. Some of your former methods of taking command of your situation simply won't be up to the job. Distractions will no longer work. Upbeat attitudes won't carry you through the day. Stark, painful realities may contradict your spiritual convictions. Hidden insecurities and fears may now reveal themselves. Profound loss forces you to consider new perspectives on the meaning of your life and why things happen the way they do. If you were rigid and withholding before, you may discover it is better now to act with a more generous spirit. If you were timid and cautious before, you may realize it is necessary to act with boldness. If you trusted easily before, you may need to be more discerning. If you mistrusted, you may now be forced to depend on others whom you do not know. If you doubted God's existence before, you may now be certain he doesn't exist—or you may see signs that perhaps God does exist. If you are someone who leads with your heart, you may encounter moments when you must lead with your fist. And if you typically lead with your fist, you may now be compelled to lead with your heart.

The Path of Release forces you to let go of some old ways of coping and grab hold of new ways of coping. That can cause you confusion but guidance and insights will be forthcoming—which is the second assurance.

Consider Mike, a martial arts teacher and an admitted control freak. He planned his days hour by hour. He believed himself to be fair-minded but the house rules for his wife and children were always his rules designed, he thought, to protect his loved ones from harm. What were his rules? They were simple. Be prepared. Plan ahead. Take charge. Never show weakness. Solve problems on your own. If he and his wife had plans to go see a movie, the plans had to be made far enough in advance. Spontaneity made him nervous. Whenever he and his family went to a restaurant, he would only sit at a corner table in full view of all the patrons. Why? Because he never wanted to be taken by surprise by anyone or anything. One big surprise for Mike came on the day his wife told him that she no longer loved him. She had grown weary of his unyielding rules. If he continued to try to control her and the children, she would end their marriage. His carefully controlled world now came crashing down around him. All of the rules he thought so important to live by seemed to rise up at once and hand in their resignations. He used all of his powers of logic and persuasion to try to get his wife to change her mind, to no avail.

He fell into a deep depression. He began to see how his need for control had ironically rendered him helpless, the very thing he had tried so desperately to avoid. His very unhappy situation had forced him into a new way of thinking. Had his life not been turned upside down by his wife's threat of divorce, he never could have been willing to change his ways because he truly believed they were right. His wife's ultimatum forced him to rethink his ways, breaking the logjam of his rigid reasoning. Happily for him, his wife appreciated the changes she saw over time and gave him and their marriage another chance. His life had to change first in order for his thinking to change.

The Second Assurance: You Will Receive Insights

Some form of insight or wisdom will come your way and help you on the rest of your journey, but only after you have battled dragons. It is in that struggle that you discover which attitudes work for you and which now work against you. Often, it is only when you lay bloodied and bruised and barely able to pick yourself up that a release occurs. A decision to let go of some old patterns of coping or some hurtful childhood memory allows you to open yourself to a greater wisdom. In his book *Pathways to Bliss*, teacher and author Joseph Campbell tells how he was lecturing to a group of students that gaining wisdom occurs only after decades of living and learning. One young lady came up to him after class to correct him.

"Mr. Campbell," she said. "You don't know much about the younger generation. We go directly from infancy to wisdom."

"That is great," he replied. "All you've missed is life."

In the great mythical stories, the hero is purposely kept in the dark about key facts in the early stages of the adventure. There was a reason Dorothy was never told early on how to tap her shoes together to get back home to Kansas, and a reason Luke Skywalker was never told from the beginning that his nemesis Darth Vader was actually his father. Heroes must be capable of making the most of the wisdom they gain as they travel through their journey; otherwise, the wisdom is pointless. They must understand why the insights are indeed wise, and then use that wisdom for a greater good. That can't happen without a fuller life experience, a journey of transformation— often preceded by loss—where they face themselves completely, perhaps for the first time.

A poignant news story that gained popular attention in December 2013 reminded me of this assurance. Brenda, a wife and mother of four boys, passed away in 2011 from ovarian cancer. A month before she died she wrote a letter to her husband David. But instead of giving the letter to David, she gave it to a close friend for safekeeping, asking her friend to mail it to a radio station known for granting Christmas wishes each December. The friend was under strict orders not to mail the letter until she was confident David had "moved on" and found a new person with whom to share his life. I never met David, but I know that, like many people, he may have struggled with his feelings about moving on after the death of a spouse. What would his four boys think? What would Brenda think? Was he being disloyal to her memory? But it is in the struggle to trust our self, our inner voice, that growth occurs. Two years after Brenda died, David finally decided that it was okay to move forward with his new life and his new partner, Jane. Any inner conflicts he may have had were resolved. The radio station called to tell him that they had a special letter for him, sent by Brenda. In her letter, Brenda listed several Christmas wishes. Her first wish was that Dave's new love be given a special day of pampering. "She deserves it," Brenda wrote, "being a stepmother to all those boys." She also wished for a magical trip for the entire family. The radio station generously arranged for them to go to Disney World. Had David received Brenda's letter before he found Jane, perhaps his decision to move on would have been easier to make. But he would have missed the opportunity to know and trust himself better, something that only happens when we grapple with conflicting wants, needs, and beliefs.

The Third Assurance: You Can Peacefully Coexist with Uncertainty

As challenging as it might be, learning to peacefully coexist with uncertainty is the only sane way to proceed on your journey. Joseph Campbell, who has written so eloquently about the hero's journey, once said that if you can see your path clearly laid out in front of you, it isn't your path. Your path is apparent only at each separate step along the way, and its ending place is unknown. You are on this journey precisely because the path you thought you were on suddenly vanished or took an unexpected turn. You once saw a path fully laid out in front of you only to discover it wasn't meant to be. When losses and tragedies happen, the unexpected road is now your new road; the once hidden path is your new path. If there is one comfort, it is that the unexpected roads are the well-traveled roads. Almost all who have come before you have walked them.

I once met a man who had fully embraced living with change and uncertainty in his everyday life. We were introduced at a workshop on intuition and spiritual development. He reminded me of the actor Orlando Bloom. In his late twenties, John had a powerful smile, a close buzzcut, and cerebral palsy. John sat in his motorized wheelchair, his movements spastic and his speech almost impossible to understand. His mother sat nearby, offering him any needed assistance and interpreting his comments for others.

The workshop had many exercises that required us to pair up or gather into small groups. I walked over and asked John if I could be his partner for an upcoming exercise. During our conversation I quickly realized that John was highly intuitive. Right off the bat he said to me, "You kept your feelings to yourself when you were a child."

"You're right," I said, surprised.

"You got that from your mother." Right again.

He proceeded to tell me more about myself, some general information, some highly specific, all accurate. I attempted to do the same for him. "I have a feeling you like to pull pranks," I said. He started to laugh, flashing me his high-wattage smile. Score one for me, I thought. He then leaned in closer, paused, and with a penetrating gaze finally said, "You're a healer." This remark touched me deeply. He didn't know I was a psychologist or that I view my vocation as one of healing, or that I was now writing a book about healing, specifically healing from loss. He didn't know these things, but still he knew.

I learned that John's closest friend had died some time ago, something that still pained him tremendously. John had few close friends. His physical challenges made it hard for him to socialize. Still, he pursued life with determination, without the slightest murmur of self-pity. He loved the dogs he cared for at home. He was very bright and he loved writing. By the time the four-day workshop ended, John had inspired everyone in attendance to not allow one's disadvantages to create doubt but instead to doubt one's disadvantages. I realized that the word "healer" best described *him*.

How does John manage to sustain his positive outlook? How does he manage through each and every day, never knowing for sure what new obstacles he will face? For that matter, how does his mother cope with what must be a full-time occupation looking after her son? How does she deal with the inevitable: that one day he will have to survive without her—or she without him? Despite their struggles, which at times are monumental, they have learned to make friends with uncertainty, to control what they can and allow the rest to unfold as it will. They release their fears of the unknown and trust that they can make the best of their uncertain future, that no matter what transpires it can help deepen their souls' longings to coexist peacefully with all that is.

The Fourth Assurance: Your Life Is Always Worthwhile

Marianne, a single mom, was totally dedicated to her only child, Susan. When Susan moved out of state to attend college,

Marianne became depressed. She believed that her sole purpose in life, raising her daughter, had come to an end and she felt lost and adrift. When she spoke to me of how they both packed the car with Susan's belongings and drove seven hours to Susan's dormitory, she could just as easily have been describing a funeral procession. She told me that after returning home that evening she gazed at one of Susan's old dolls sitting on a shelf in her bedroom, and that to her it looked forlorn, as if it missed its owner. I decided to use an exercise I found in the book *You Own the Power* by Rosemary Altea.

"The way you tell it, that's a very sad story," I said. "Now I'd like you to tell me a very happy story, the happiest you can recall. But there's one catch. It must be the same story you just told me."

Marianne stared at me, bewildered. She then struggled to tell her story with this new, happy twist. In less than a minute her tone changed from sullen to upbeat. Describing her daughter waving goodbye from the dorm room, Marianne no longer charged the image with deep pangs of loss; now she added a sense of excitement at her daughter's new adventure. The doll on the shelf reminded her of joyous memories of play and laughter. Within minutes Marianne discovered that her emotions had nothing to do with what had happened, but everything to do with how she had cultivated the story about what had happened.

Along the Path of Release, you finally realize that a new you is in the process of being born. Such a birth, unasked for but inevitable, is in your soul's best interest. It becomes easier to achieve if you embrace your past and present with gratitude. If you resist this birth, you will walk the alternate path, the Path of Despair.

The Path of Despair

You will discover that along the Path of Release, at some point, that path merges into the Path of Despair for a bit. The paths blend together because most people resist letting go of their former ways of thinking and coping until they fall into a hopeless despair. Only then do they realize that transformation is the only way out.

Ken had an important job in finance, was aggressively driven to succeed as far as possible, and had little patience for anything that slowed him down. He had experienced his share of losses in life. His dad died when he was a boy, so Ken had to "grow up fast" to help his mother run the household. He admitted that his impatience was at its worst while driving, since he had no tolerance for slow-pokes, often pounding his fist on the steering wheel when traffic slowed to a crawl. He told me that he tried many times to learn patience but that it just wasn't in his nature to be mellow when things weren't going his way.

But Ken did change his ways, virtually overnight. He had been driving home on a Friday night during rush hour. He had plans for the weekend—dinner with a client that night, golf with his best friend Jim the next day—and was eager to get the weekend started. What he expected to be a sixty-minute trip had stretched into nearly three hours. A heavy rain had slowed traffic and then a car accident caused traffic to come to a complete standstill as police and rescue vehicles blocked the road. Cars were backed up for ten miles. As he finally passed the site of the accident, road crews were sweeping up broken glass. The car involved in the accident sat off to the side, crushed and twisted. He shook his head at the carelessness of the driver who surely did not survive such a horrific crash. When Ken finally arrived home he was still furious that the long delay had ruined his evening plans. An hour later his phone rang and the caller ID showed that it was his friend Jim. But the voice on the other end wasn't Jim's, it was Jim's sister. She had awful news: Jim was dead. As she explained the details, Ken realized in horror and shame that the man who caused the traffic delays, the man whose car was crushed by the side of the road, the man he blamed for ruining his evening, was his best friend Jim.

"I'm no longer the same person I was before that night," Ken told me quietly. "I don't get impatient anymore. I rarely get annoyed at anything. I was in such a state of despair after Jim died, I couldn't bear being that angry person any longer. So I changed. And the change was almost instantaneous."

When despair deepens, you feel more helpless, more alone—adrift at sea with no wind, no rudder, and often no will to steer. At the lowest point of despair, practically everyone believes *"I will not survive."* Some refer to their physical survival but in most cases what they really mean is that the "I" they've identified with all their life will die. And that is true in some ways. Ken's story is a good example. But in nature, rebirth follows death. That rebirth can occur from positive events, too. Many people completely change their priorities and outlook on life once they have children. Still, most transformations happen as a result of suffering and sacrifice. When the loss is profound, many people believe that their continued existence is empty of purpose and meaning. It is only when they finally scream *"What am I supposed to do the rest of my life?"* that hope flickers in the dying embers of despair. You don't ask such a question unless you believe somewhere in the deeper recesses of your soul that hope exists for a purposeful life. Once hope appears, the paths of Despair and Release, which had temporarily merged, begin to separate.

You leave the Path of Despair completely when you restore hope. Hope is a precursor to trust and leads you back on the Path of Release. There you give up your need to control all outcomes and instead surrender peacefully to uncertainty.

Embracing Hope

Hope is bittersweet. When hope lifts your spirits, it embraces you as a friend. When hope disappoints, it taunts you as an adversary. It inspires you to imagine what's possible for you to find, and at the same time causes you to remember what you've already lost. The key to a helpful, healing form of hope is emotional acceptance, which was your first path along your journey of transformation. When you are desperate for a certain outcome, when you dread that it may not happen, any hope you muster is felt as an ache in the pit of your stomach. But when you surrender to your current reality and say, *"I don't like my situation as it is right now, but I accept it,"* you let go of your resistance. Hope rises inside you and settles as warmth in your heart. No longer reflecting a desperate wish, hope reflects the heartening possibilities.

You experience hope when you:

1. Surrender reasonable control
2. Seek understanding from one other person
3. Practice self-acceptance
4. Discover meaning and purpose to your life

Surrender Control

There is a difference between giving up in despair—*"I can't do this anymore"*—and surrendering in hope—*"I can't do this anymore by myself."* Surrendering in hope is not giving up; it is looking up. It is a willingness to ask for help, allowing what you cannot control to unfold in its own way and time. It is the recognition that the unseen world can support you in the seen world. Unwilling to tolerate uncertainty and ambiguity, unable to accept that life is full of unexpected events, you are not free. You are imprisoned by the need to know and the compulsion to find answers when no answers are forthcoming. Surrender your ego and inspiration will flow.

Controlling a specific outcome requires that we attach our ego to that outcome. The opposite is to surrender in hope, detaching our ego from outcomes. It is reasonable to want to achieve future goals. It is necessary to try to persevere through challenges. But when your life is turned upside down, when a major illness sends you reeling, when someone you love is no longer with you, your original life plans no longer matter or perhaps are no longer even possible. You are forced to take a new road where your new journey begins, the outcome of which is never knowable in advance.

Surrendering in hope means to peacefully coexist with uncertainty. The more you try to reduce or eliminate uncertainty by overthinking situations over which you have no real control, the more inner turmoil you create. Just when you think you have successfully reduced uncertainty, your mind might say, *"How do I know for sure? What if I'm wrong?"* And the fruitless endeavor to eliminate uncertainty will continue again and again.

We tend to think that when bad things happen they are, well, just bad. But what if some bad things prevent other, even

worse things from happening? We've all heard stories of someone inadvertently avoiding a terrible event by being in a different place than he usually would have been. Keep your mind
open to the possibility that your loss might actually have spared
you another misfortune.

Seek Understanding

If there is any solace for us when we walk along roads we
never wanted to travel, it is that so many others have walked
these roads before us and survived. Sitting with a friend who is
going through a major crisis or loss can be the most comforting
and hopeful thing one can do. Platitudes don't help, but simply showing up and showing that you care—just "being with"
someone in pain—does. One woman who was comforted
by friends after the death of her husband said, "I knew they
couldn't change anything that had happened. They didn't have
to. But by sitting with me, I knew how much they cared. And
I realized that as bad as things were, there was still something
good to hold on to."

Marla also found solace in shared company after a car accident seriously damaged her left leg. "Morning to night, day
after day, all I did was pray for a miracle," Marla said. She finally
ran out of hope when her doctors told her that her leg had to
be amputated. "One day I was a whole person, the next day I
was a person with one leg. How would I go on with my life?"
she thought. When she underwent physical therapy and was fit-
ted for a prosthetic leg, she had the opportunity to see people
of all ages undergoing the same kind of challenge.

"When I saw that they still could smile after all they had
been through I began to feel hopeful again," she said. "Hopeful

that I could get through this and still find a way to be happy. If they could do it, I could do it too."

Dr. Kenneth Doka's book *Disenfranchised Grief* reveals that the grief some people experience is not recognized by society, so they rarely receive much support and understanding. Some situations don't automatically generate the kind of condolences you might need: the death of your ex-spouse, the loss of your longtime pet, your sudden miscarriage, or your best friend's move across the country. Or imagine grieving the death of a grandparent you felt immeasurably close to, only to be told by a coworker, "At least it wasn't your mother." Knowing that someone understands your grief gives you hope that you can get through it. If you don't receive that understanding, you are lacking the support you need to heal.

Sometimes in your wish to be understood, you may need to ask others to simply listen as carefully as they can—without offering advice, or a quick fix, or cheery forecasts. Having someone listen to you without judgment may be all you need to notice a calming sense of release and to feel a little more hopeful once again. Good listeners allow you to actually hear yourself speak. When your words are out in the open instead of rattling around inside your head, you can sort through the fears, the exaggerations, and the multiple layers of meanings hidden behind what you say to discern what you truly think and believe. Having someone there to listen wholeheartedly allows you to feel cared about, too. When you don't feel so alone, therein lies the flicker of hope.

Lindsay had a brain tumor. Her doctors told her that surgery would be necessary and though urgent, she had time to plan ahead. She and her husband Don read all of the information they could get their hands on about her type of tumor and what to expect during recovery. Though her outlook was very good, there was—as with any surgery—always the danger of impairment, incapacitation, or even death. When Lindsay's trusted surgeon told her he would not be available to perform the operation, she had to find a new surgeon. She interviewed various doctors only to come away with a deepening sense of dread. One doctor was so cold and clinical that she could not relate to him at all. Another seemed more engaging but he recommended a course of aftercare totally different from what all of the previous doctors had suggested. Through the months of preplanning, her husband Don gave Lindsay unwavering support, always remaining upbeat. He never sounded worried, always had a reassuring word to offer. Lindsay knew he was trying to be helpful but sometimes he made her feel that he didn't really understand the depth of her worries. When she asked him how he managed to stay so calm and optimistic, he simply stated that he knew matters would work out so there was nothing to really be worried about.

One morning, Don suggested that they go see a movie right after her medical appointment scheduled for that afternoon. Lindsay, very anxious about the upcoming appointment and increasingly frightened at the prospect of brain surgery, was astonished that Don seemed so casual, even indifferent. "I have to have a craniotomy and all you can think about is going to a movie?" she scolded. She wasn't prepared for his reaction.

Don broke down crying, sobbing for minutes on end, barely able to speak. When he finally did get his words out, he told her how frightened he was that he might lose her and that he couldn't stand the thought of life without her. All along he had tried to be strong for her but inwardly he had been petrified. That revelation created a huge, positive shift for them both. Lindsay had always regarded herself as a strong person, but the fear of brain surgery made her feel weak. Now she knew that as much as she needed Don's support, he needed her too. That gave her the strength she thought she had lost. "We felt even closer after that," Lindsay said. "And more hopeful." Actually, releasing fears doesn't give you hope. It allows the hope that already exists to reveal itself.

Practice Self-Acceptance

During times of trauma and tragedy, it is an almost universal reaction to regret one's actions. Sometimes we blame ourselves for what happened, or for not preventing it in the first place. Other times we regret our past actions when we were less kind or thoughtful than we should have been to someone, now that it's too late to make amends. It is fine to take a moral inventory and decide what needs improving, but when suffering a major loss, we often beat ourselves up so much that we lose hope in ourselves. The effect is compounded when old, unfavorable messages about us from childhood interact with our own negative self-evaluations.

That is not so much a problem of low self-esteem as it is a problem of low self-acceptance. If you suffer from low self-esteem, you will find it hard to talk yourself into feeling good unless you already accept yourself—and accept both your good qualities and your not-so-good ones. Otherwise any positive thought you might have had about yourself will eventually be followed by a negative thought to counter it. Without self-acceptance, building self-esteem is like building a house of cards that is bound to collapse.

Phil encountered this situation after a car accident left his wife Paula in a coma. He had been by her side for thirty-six hours when the doctors told him to go home and rest. Paula was doing as well as could be expected and there was nothing more that could be done medically. Now it was a waiting game.

Phil returned home but found it hard to sleep. He decided to keep busy by tidying up the house. He had always found it annoying that Paula created clutter in their home, holding on to old books, magazines, and boxes from home deliveries. Eventually they would get thrown out but Paula always first resisted, thinking she might find a use for them later on. Now was his chance, he thought, to get rid of it all. But he couldn't do it. As much as he complained to Paula about the clutter, he now felt guilty for having made all those complaints. He started thinking negative thoughts, making a mental list of everything about himself he disliked. By the time he finished his list, he was more depressed than ever. He started to imagine the worst happening, that Paula wouldn't survive, and he wondered how such a miserable person as himself could ever be happy again.

Exercise: Positive Self-Analysis

This type of negative self-analysis only leads to more feelings of guilt and sadness. If you find yourself in this mindset, try to complement it by coming up with an alternate list of things you like about yourself. Then make a distinction between guilt and regret. Guilt says *"I'm bad."* Regret says *"I wish I had done things differently but I'm a good person."*

I wrote earlier that the Path of Acceptance is the foundational pathway. It is essential that you learn to accept yourself if you are to eventually find inner peace. Your faults, your weaknesses, your mistakes, your annoying habits or personality quirks may not be flattering, but they deserve to be acknowledged and accepted as much as your favorable qualities. If you don't, one of two things will happen: you will deny or minimize your flaws and therefore not be able to change them when needed, or you will emphasize your flaws so much that you will overlook your strengths when they are needed. Either way, your ability to cope well during adversity will be compromised and your trust in yourself and in your future will dwindle.

Try to Discover Meaning in Your Situation

My daughter's good friend Michael was teaching school in China as part of a two-year program. He loved his work and he loved his students but every day he missed his friends and family. As his first Christmas away from home approached, he felt even more lonesome. One afternoon he found a letter on his desk, handwritten by one of his young students, along with a perfect red apple. Pictures of snowmen decorated the letter and the imperfect grammar made him chuckle. "How heartfelt," he thought. It was everything a person far from home could ask for. Here is part of the letter:

Teacher Michael,

Happy Christmas Day! I know that you want come home this year. I also feel sad. But you will not be alone you have many students. Christmas day seems a very important day in America. In that day people come home and have a great time with their family. This year Christmas day I want to give you some warm. So I write this card. Every day you must happy. All the class six's students are love you forever. Best Wishes.

For a lonely young American man teaching in China it would not be unexpected for his heart to ache for those people and things he missed. And yet the simple words on a single piece of paper written by a young boy struggling with a strange new language let him know that his sacrifices were important, worthwhile, and meaningful. They inspired hope in him that he would make it through his journey and be enriched for it.

To nurture hope during trying times, you need to believe that your suffering is meaningful and, more important, that your life is meaningful. This requires that your lower-self needs for safety, security, achievement, and control give way to higher-self values.

After the stock market crashed in 1929, some men jumped to their deaths believing, once their wealth was gone, that life was no longer worth living. As some people age, become infirm, and outlive many of their loved ones, they start to believe that their purpose in life no longer exists. They then live out their days in quiet despair. We often hear the phrase "quality of life" as it pertains to end-of-life issues. Some feel that it is perhaps a blessing that a person with Alzheimer's or with some other severe disability dies, since their quality of life was so limited. But how you determine a quality life depends on which values you rely upon—lower-self or higher-self values. If a person loses the capacity to be productive or experience pleasure, if a person is bedridden or no longer possesses sound mental faculties, that person might be regarded as having a poor quality of life according to lower-self values that emphasize comfort, control, and productivity. But we also aspire to higher values such as generous love, compassion, and forgiveness. Our higher self has the capacity to appreciate beauty, to be in awe of nature or the experience of life itself, or to seek a deeper connection to God. People who are very ill, even slowly dying, are still capable of extending love, offering forgiveness, praying for others, being an inspiration, or deepening their religious faith. Those are not low-quality values but the stuff of our souls. And if a person is totally disabled or unaware, it becomes a precious opportunity for others to show love and caring to that individual. Love and sacrifice is beneficial to the giver as well as the receiver.

The Final Path

The hardships and losses you have faced forced you onto a road you weren't expecting to travel. In the process you released some of your old-self illusions in order for a new self to be born. But any lessons learned, any wisdom gained will mean very little unless you look beyond yourself to others in need. The Path of Compassion awaits you, as does its counterpart the Path of Emptiness. We have come this far together. Let me guide you the rest of the way.

CHAPTER 6

The Path of Compassion

"How far you go in life depends on your being tender with the young, compassionate with the aged, sympathetic with the striving and tolerant of the weak and strong. Because someday in your life you will have been all of these."

—GEORGE WASHINGTON CARVER

—— Finding Peace Together ——

"Sometimes I would watch the news on TV. I'd see people despairing over the loss of loved ones from so many terrible events. And I did not care," Pamela said. "My daughter was gone forever. That was all that mattered to me." She took a photo out of her purse of her daughter hugging their sheepdog. Danielle, a beautiful college student, had a genetic heart defect no one knew existed. One day her heart simply stopped. "I had tried so many times to pull myself out of my grief but nothing worked," Pamela said.

"One sunny afternoon I was sitting outside in my garden, miserable as always, when my dog Annabelle, the one in the photo, came over to me. She opened her mouth wide and I was amazed to see, cradled gently on her tongue, a baby bird with an injured wing. Annabelle carefully placed the bird on the ground, then looked up at me as if to say 'Well? Don't you think you should do something? This bird needs our help!' I know it sounds crazy, but at that moment I realized I needed to get beyond my own pain and do something to help others. So I took the bird to the vet and they showed me how to nurse it back to health. A week later I told the daughter of a good friend, this story of my dog Annabelle. Anna, whose name is similar to my dog's, told me that the name Anna means 'grace.' I saw that as a sign. I think it was grace from God that Annabelle showed me what I needed to do. And I know Danielle would be proud."

Even when brokenhearted, you can still experience some solace, some sense of peace, when you act with compassion toward others in need. The first three Paths of Transformation that you traveled compelled you to reach inward, to discover more about yourself. The final path requires you to reach outward, to discover more about others—allowing you to rediscover yourself.

The Path of Compassion

You have suffered through days of pain and loss. You've struggled to pick yourself up after falling. Your body weakens. You wonder why you had to go through these ordeals. Why fall in love if you end up alone or brokenhearted? Why raise a child if that child dies tragically young? Why aspire to a career if illness, injury, or bad luck kills your dream? Why work hard if it can all be taken from you in a flash? The purpose of your journey is to make meaningful all of your life experiences, the bitter and the sweet. It is to find a reason for living in the midst of heartache and loss.

You plant the seed of meaningfulness when you realize that in spite of your suffering—and even *because* of your suffering—you can experience a meaningful quality of life. It is the possibility that you have much to offer life; that you can make a difference not only in the lives of people you know and love but those you have yet to meet. Life may be beautiful or not when you stand back and observe it from a distance, but it becomes meaningful when you extend yourself in the service of others. "No man is an island unto himself." You are part of a large mosaic. The tribulations or losses you've experienced may have seemed senseless, but the sufferings you've endured will not be. A family whose teenage son dies in a car accident might start a scholarship fund for needy children in the young man's honor. A recovering alcoholic in AA might donate time to sponsor another person in the program. A woman whose mother died of breast cancer might commit to a charity walk, earning money for cancer research. Anyone who has been saddened by loss and offers a smile and a word of encouragement to someone in grief gives the message "I made it through and you will, too."

Jay realized he had more to offer the world after his wife of fifty years died following a long battle with illness. Jay had spent the last two years in lonely isolation, believing that his life no longer had meaning. One day he forced himself to go for a walk into town. "I had no real reason to leave the house that day. I'm still not sure what got me to go out," he said.

Heading downtown, he waited to cross a busy intersection when a woman with three small children walked up beside him. "I looked at that young mother and thought back to when my wife was also a young mother with a couple of rambunctious kids." Suddenly, the littlest boy, maybe three years old, broke free of his mother's hand and began to run onto the road into the path of an oncoming car. "Without even thinking I stepped onto the road, quickly grabbed the boy and pulled him back to safety. The mother was so profusely thankful it almost embarrassed me. She told me I saved her son's life. As I walked home I wondered what would have happened had I not been there. Then I realized something else. My life had lost meaning for me but on that one day my life had meaning to that mother and especially to her little boy. It got me thinking, maybe my life still had a purpose after all," Jay revealed.

Sympathy vs. Empathy

There is a difference between sympathy and empathy. Sympathy is when you feel bad about someone's hardship. Sometimes, sympathy includes a negative judgment: "I feel sorry for you and your situation but you made some bad choices." A sympathetic response often falls short of a full understanding of what the other person is experiencing and why. It is often accompanied by well-intended but hasty urges to get the person to look on the bright side of the situation. Saying "I'm sorry your Mom died, but at least she isn't suffering anymore" may be factually correct but the underlying message is, "Don't feel too bad about your mother dying."

Empathy, which is more profound, is possible only when a person possesses a deeper and broader understanding of the other person's pain. Walking in another's shoes, an empathic person literally feels the pain of the sufferer or recalls his or her own similar pain. An empathic person becomes vulnerable to pain in order to become a healing presence. Empathy creates a shared experience and a strong sense of connection. Empathy is without judgment; it does not try to talk anyone out of their pain—as if that were even possible.

Compassion builds on empathy by taking it one step further. It turns an inner feeling into an outward action. It might be a simple and heartfelt "I'm so sorry that your Mom died" followed by a willingness to "be" with that person or offer assistance in some practical way.

Compassion is an aspect of love, but some loving acts, while self-sacrificing, seem to lack emotion or passion. Sometimes in relationships, the feelings of love come and go but the commitment to act lovingly remains. Some days you go through the motions of love even when you don't feel all that loving. It is not being inauthentic; it is human. You are simply allowing higher-self states of devotion, understanding, and forgiveness to rule over lower-self desires. Consider these examples:

- Your head says "I'm tired"—your heart says "I must get out of bed and check on my child anyway."
- Your head says "How dare she talk that way to me!"—your heart says "She must be having a bad day, maybe she needs a hug."
- Your head says "You wronged me"—your heart says "I forgive you."
- Your head says "Life is unfair to me"—your heart says "Look at all I have been given that brings me true joy."

- Your head says "I am right, you're wrong"—your heart says "Help me to understand you better."
- Your head says "I am charitable enough"—your heart says "Help me to see where I am falling short."

Recognize Yourself in Others

Genuine compassion for others does not come from pity, even when a person is experiencing a loss. It comes from the deep awareness that we are all connected, that the stranger you meet on the road is you in disguise, that everyone has his or her own cross to bear and arduous journey to travel. No one who has lived long enough or loved hard enough has avoided suffering. The Good Samaritan helps the wounded man on the road in part because he recognizes himself in the fallen traveler. Mother Teresa and her Missionaries of Charity aided the poorest of the poor in Kolkata, India: feeding the hungry, sheltering the homeless, caring for and comforting those near death. She said her task was never a burden because she saw Jesus in everyone.

The Power of Compassion

All of us have material needs that must be met if we are to survive physically. But we also have nonmaterial needs that must be met if we are to survive spiritually. Our higher-self spiritual needs are these: unselfish love, the release of fears, and a purposeful life. I asked myself if there is an experience in which all three of these are simultaneously present. The one that came instantly to mind was this: when, without forethought for risks, we rush to provide comfort or aid to someone in danger or who is being threatened. It could be as dramatic as risking one's life to save another, or risking one's reputation for one who has been maligned. In such moments, the "I" or "me" no longer exists. Instead, it is "we."

Here's a dramatic example of "we." Two young girls watched in horror as their fifty-year-old construction worker father leaped onto a New York City subway track. Wesley Autrey jumped onto the tracks to rescue a young film student who had fallen there after suffering a seizure. The oncoming train was so close there was no time to lift the stricken man to safety, so Mr. Autrey pressed his body on top of the young man, squeezing them both into a space barely a foot high. The train rolled over them, inches above Mr. Autrey's head. Amazingly, both men survived with no serious injuries. Later, Autrey told the *New York Times*, "I don't feel like I did something spectacular; I just saw someone who needed help. I did what I felt was right." Autrey was dubbed "The Subway Samaritan" and his selfless act made headlines worldwide.

The Risk in Judging Others

Philosopher Martin Buber described what he called the "I-Thou" relationship whereby we relate to other people in a manner that recognizes their sacredness. When we objectify others, disregard their humanity, or see them as "less-than" we engage in what he called an "I-It" relationship. On the Path of Compassion, you become aware of what you have in common with all of humanity and begin to relate to others as "Thou" instead of as "It." Imagine you are in a grocery store standing in a checkout line. The man in front of you, sighing loudly, makes rude comments about the slowness of the line. What might you think of that person? You have choices. You don't know the facts of his life—his background, attitudes, or social standing. But you can imagine that he has longings and fears, or has suffered loss or disappointment. Even if you never speak a word to him, you have a choice to cultivate goodwill, ill will, or indifference.

While waiting for her flight, a woman in the airport lounge buys a novel and a bag of her favorite cookies. A man is sitting two chairs down from her and the bag of cookies sits on the chair between them. Engrossed in her novel, she begins to eat her cookies. The man reaches into the same bag and also begins eating the cookies. The woman—too horrified to speak—pulls the bag closer to her. The man reaches over again and takes another cookie. She thinks to herself, *"How incredibly rude!"* Finally, there is one last cookie. The man reaches into the bag, takes the cookie, breaks it in two and offers her half. She looks at him in disgust, turning her head away. Finally, boarding the plane, she is glad to be rid of this bizarre man. Once in her seat she opens her purse—and in there she sees her unopened bag of cookies, right where she first left it.

How often are we convinced we know the truth? How often do we react with indignation when others challenge our cherished beliefs? How often do we accuse others of something of which we are also guilty? How often do we insist on being right when being kind is a better alternative? When we act with compassion we suspend judgments of who is right and who is wrong and simply offer a helping hand.

The Path of Compassion cannot end your heartbreak but it can help mend your heart. Showing concern for others who can use your help, sharing the wisdom you gained along your journey, adds meaning to your tribulations and nurtures the inner peace you long for. If you are battle-worn, scarred, or angry, acts of compassion may seem too much for you right now. That is when, at least for a while, you will walk the Path of Emptiness.

The Path of Emptiness

Great mythic stories of heroic journeys begin when something precious is threatened or lost and the hero must undertake a quest to find a treasure that will end the threat or find what was lost. In the King Arthur tales, it was the quest for the Holy Grail. In *The Wizard of Oz* it was the search for the wizard so Dorothy could get back to Kansas. In *The Lord of the Rings* Frodo seeks the fires of Mount Doom to destroy the ring of power and save the land from evil. But, as author Carol Pearson points out in her book *Awakening the Heroes Within,* in all such journeys—especially your own—the sought-after treasure is actually one's true self. Once that treasure is found, the journey becomes pointless unless two things happen:

1. The hero must use the wisdom that was gained for some greater good.
2. The underlying motivation must be for the sake of others rather than for the hero's own sake.

Compassion is thwarted when you filter your desire to help others through your lower-self needs for security, esteem, and control rather than the higher-self desires to offer care, love, and assistance. Compassionate acts done primarily to gain personal power, appreciation, or recognition—acts filtered through your ego—do not possess the same healing power as acts motivated by the pure desire to alleviate another's pain. Noble-appearing acts done for less than noble reasons provide short-term relief at best. Pure compassion, based on love, is devotional, not self-serving. It possesses power because it is not hampered by personal fears or desires. It flows naturally from you because you see your connection to all living things. You understand that suffering is a natural part of life and that helping to heal the suffering of others is also a necessary part of life. Your demonstration of compassion is revealed through acts of generosity, self-sacrifice, and devotional love.

Along the Path of Emptiness any compassion you might offer stops short of true devotion. You ask yourself questions such as *"Why should I put myself out for others? What did they ever do for me? Why can't someone else do this? How will this benefit me? How will this affect my life, my reputation? How do I know it's worth the effort?"* As you defend and make excuses, you allow fears and personal desires—aspects of your lower self—to once again run your life.

Under ordinary circumstances, people find it easier to show compassion for others if three conditions are met:

1. Their suffering is severe.
2. Their suffering is not self-inflicted.
3. Their suffering is due to something with which people can identify.

Those conditions represent subjective value judgments that actually limit your opportunities to show compassion. While you might show compassion to someone who is seriously injured in a car accident not their fault, you might not show compassion to someone seriously injured because they were driving drunk. However, when you have suffered through a major loss or life-altering event and traveled the Four Paths of Transformation—the Path of Acceptance, the Path of Inspiration, the Path of Release, and the Path of Compassion—you will more readily offer compassion to someone in pain even if the three conditions are not fully met. Once transformed, you open your eyes to what unites you to others—not what separates you—and then you open your heart to embrace them.

True acts of compassion bring healing to others and also heal the healer. What you do for others you do for yourself. And the good you withhold from others you withhold from yourself. Perhaps the most noble act of compassion—short of actually risking one's life for another person—is the decision to forgive those who have deeply hurt you.

The Quest to Forgive

If the loss you're experiencing is due to an affair or betrayal, you face another challenge: managing your relationship with the person in question. Affairs, lies, and poor decisions in relationships can create a profound loss in trust. If there is to be a true reconciliation, forgiving the person's misdeeds is the difficult but necessary choice.

Marjorie learned this firsthand. Her heart had sunk when she read the text on her husband's phone. There was no mistake. Her husband Michael was carrying on an affair with a coworker and it had been going on for at least four months. When she confronted him with the overwhelming evidence, he confessed. Over the course of many months, desperate to win back her trust and love, Michael expressed sincere remorse. Like many betrayed partners, Marjorie asked countless questions, never quite believing he had told her the whole truth, never quite believing she could trust him ever again. After eight exhausting months of endless debates, marathon discussions, and conversations that would drag on into the night, Marjorie believed that forgiving Michael was next to impossible. A black cloud hung over their relationship.

The process of reconciliation after an affair involves many factors that need to be untangled and addressed, usually over a long period of time. But in all cases of betrayal, the most important and most difficult task for the one betrayed has less to do with facing the truth of what happened and more to do with facing the truth of oneself. In order to forgive, the one betrayed must examine his or her ego, fears, and insecurities, and ultimately discover a way to transcend lower-self fears by embracing higher-self values.

Dr. Robert Enright is one of the leading researchers in the scientific study of forgiveness and author of *Forgiveness Is a Choice*. He found that the forgiveness proceeds through four phases: the uncovering phase, the decision phase, the work phase, and the release phase.

The Uncovering Phase

Affairs often devastate the betrayed partner because they strike at the heart of a person's lower-self fears: loss of lovability, loss of esteem, loss of security, and loss of control. Marjorie now felt unloved, inadequate, unsafe, and no longer in control of her life. She needed to uncover the depth of her hurt and anger. She needed to look deep within herself. Had she ever felt this way before? Were there old hurts getting in the way of overcoming the new hurts?

Marjorie felt humiliated by Michael's affair. When anyone is shamed or humiliated, they tend to view the guilty party as the sole cause of all the pain they feel and the problems they face. It is only through a process of self-discovery that the wounded person realizes that part of the reason they are suffering has to do with their own insecurities and self-doubts activated by the betrayal. Make no mistake: the wounding person needs to closely examine his or her own insecurities and flaws. But the wounded person will move closer toward healing when he or she is able to look inward as well. This is usually very difficult too soon after a betrayal but becomes more possible over time. The Dalai Lama has said that being aware of a single shortcoming within oneself is more useful than being aware of a thousand shortcomings in someone else.

The Decision Phase

If you wish to reconcile, you must choose to forgive even if you don't feel like forgiving. Forgiveness begins as an intellectual choice before it is a felt desire. The decision to forgive is often made because everything else that has been tried has failed to alleviate the suffering. Often this decision to forgive is made reluctantly because it doesn't seem fair to forgive. "At first when I decided to forgive him, I felt like I was letting him get away with something," Marjorie said. But at this phase Marjorie also realized that she needed to let go of her understandable desire to take revenge. "I'd punish him in countless ways," she said. "I'd ignore him, criticize him, push him away, and refuse to be happy around him. But I knew I had to let go of all of that if we were to ever get past this."

The Work Phase

The next step is to overcome the obstacles to forgiveness. Marjorie discovered that her main obstacles to forgiveness had been her own insecurities—questioning her lovability and attractiveness—not just the betrayal by her husband.

"I consider myself a very good cook," she said. "Last week I brought one of my favorite dishes to a potluck lunch meeting and I overheard one coworker whisper to another that she didn't like what I had made. But it didn't bother me, because no matter what she thought, I knew I was a great cook. And that got me thinking. Why was I so devastated by Michael's infidelity? Maybe deep down I didn't believe I was so lovable or desirable. If I had thought better about myself before this happened, would I have been able to get past it by now?"

In the work phase, you broaden your perspective. You don't look for reasons to excuse what happened but try to better understand why it happened—and that "why" includes the deeper reasons of why you reacted the way you did. You see both yourself and the one who hurt you as possessing strengths and flaws. Emotional injuries can and do create insecurities but they also reveal the insecurities that already exist. Everyone has a "shadow" self.

- Your **negative shadow** represents unflattering aspects that have remained hidden from your awareness, denied in yourself but often readily seen in others. The more harshly you judge others, the more you are overlooking some aspect of yourself.
- Your **positive shadow** represents noble potentials that you suppressed but see more readily in others. Perhaps the more you deeply admire someone's abilities or accomplishments, the more you are suppressing some inner strength.

You may battle forces outside of yourself—a boring job, a loveless relationship, a disease, or a life without someone you love—but your real battle is ultimately within. You discover opposing desires and fears inside yourself: a fear of forgiving and a fear of remaining bitter; a fear of taking a risk and a fear of playing it safe; a fear of self-discovery and a fear of self-delusion; a fear of losing your former life and a fear of never finding a new life. As the battle rages and you proceed down the transformational paths of Acceptance, Inspiration, and Release, you have the opportunity to move past the dualistic, either/or ways of thinking. Questions such as *"Am I this type of person or that type of person?"* or *"Do I believe in this or do I believe in that?"* then become resolved by your realizing that it is never one or the other but both. You are always one thing *and* another. You are many things all rolled into one, including aspects you had suppressed. It is only when you acknowledge and accept the hidden sides of yourself that they can be managed better. On the Path of Compassion you now realize that everyone has a shadow side, everyone has fears and insecurities, and everyone can be blind to who they really are until they travel their own journey of transformation. It is in your journey on the Path of Compassion that you see how you are similar to others, and how you will need forgiveness as well.

"I told myself that I would never have done to Michael what he did to me," Marjorie said. "And I truly believe that—although one never knows for sure. But I also believe that Michael is fundamentally a good person. He is flawed and inse-cure. But so am I. He wounded me deeply. And in the past eight months I've repeatedly wounded him by rejecting and condemning him. Is he worth forgiving? I am worth forgiving, so how can I say that he is not?"

Thinking better of the offender or at least wishing him or her well is also part of this phase. You need not feel as warmly toward the offender as Marjorie was starting to feel toward Michael. Simply thinking *"I hope one day they see the error of their ways"* might be enough.

Finally, the hurt must be accepted and absorbed. The cycle of pain and unfairness must stop.

The Release Phase

Here you accept the idea that suffering is both an inevitable and an essential part of life. The nature of your suffering and loss forces your strengths to come forth and your weaknesses to be revealed. It is under those circumstances that you can change yourself and thus change the course of your future.

The nature of your adversity and your response to it can provide clues to the deeper purpose of your life. It is through struggle and turmoil that you discover what you value most and how you want to reflect this in your life. You might become someone who takes up the fight for a social cause or be an advocate for those suffering from certain illnesses. All compassionate people have suffered but they then used their suffering to comfort the afflicted, soothe pain, and restore hope. You never know when your act of compassion will make the difference in a person's life. When someone is on the brink of despair, a loving gesture can be the one thing they desperately need in order to trust that all is not lost.

"Forgiving Michael changed me for the better," Marjorie said. "I don't feel as self-absorbed as I once did. I realize that I have the power and the opportunity to make everyone's life a little bit brighter if I think compassionate thoughts rather than judgmental ones."

Self-Forgiveness

Showing compassion for yourself is necessary during grief. Grief often involves painful self-recriminations—guilt and regrets—that halt the process of inner peace. Forgiveness starts that process back up and is a key part of the Path of Compassion.

Self-forgiveness begins with accepting that you have made mistakes and are not perfect. Berating yourself for failures is a refusal to accept that you were never designed to be perfect. You were designed to give and receive love despite your imperfections. If you lack compassion for yourself, does that mean you will lack compassion for others? Many of my clients act loving and compassionate toward others but they are much harder on themselves. *"Can I truly love others if I don't love myself?"* they wonder. The truth is simple: if you extend love or compassion toward another it is because on a soul level you understand that you and the other are united. Love for another is self-love projected outward. There is no distinction between self-directed love and other-directed love. There is only love.

You Are Worthy of Love

The belief that you do not love yourself enough can be understood, on a psychological level, as love that gets filtered first through your lower-self fears rather than your higher-self values. Imagine you are drinking water through a straw. The water represents love. If you show a great deal of love and compassion for others, you are drinking through a very wide straw. If you show less love and compassion for yourself, then you have switched to a very thin straw. Now you will drink only a small amount of water. Your lower-self fears don't filter out love. They alter your ability to fully experience the love that is already there.

Steve doubted his worthiness and lovability. Shy and sensitive, he was delighted when Dawn showed an interest in him. He quickly became devoted to her, showering her with attention and gifts. Over time he grew to genuinely love her but his insecurities stayed close to the surface of their relationship. When she didn't respond quickly to his text messages, he worried that perhaps she had lost interest in him. He started to require more and more reassurances from her that she loved him. Eventually Dawn grew weary of having to constantly prove her love and she withdrew. That caused him to fear the worst—he was indeed not worth loving.

What if Steve had believed right from the start that he was worthy of love? Would he have acted differently? Perhaps on some occasions he wouldn't have acted so over-the-top. The main difference, though, is that those loving acts would not have been filtered through fear, motivated by a need to prove his worthiness. Rather, he would be motivated by care and love, a reflection of the love that already existed within him. He would also accept the possibility that despite their love for one another, they might not choose to stay together. When filtered through higher-self values, love is not possessive. He would also trust that love exists without it having to be proven daily. The worry and anxiety that accompanies mistrust of another is really mistrust in your ability to manage your emotions or your life if you are betrayed.

Conquer Doubt

Lower-self fears ignite internal debate and conflict. You try to counter your good qualities by pointing out your not-so-good qualities. But verbal persuasion and logic fails to calm lower-self fears, eventually causing you to ask *"What if I'm wrong?"* or *"How do I know for sure?"* These questions once again ignite self-doubt. It is only when you break this cycle, reach for higher-self values—and cross over the bridge to the Path of Acceptance—that you stop the debates. On that bridge you begin to accept yourself as a mix of qualities and understand that personal growth comes from facing fears head-on. Growth comes from believing in your innate worthiness no matter what the circumstances. Your higher self believes that you are the incarnation of love and that your job is to reveal that love and not diminish it through fears. That requires trust and courage.

The chasm between your belief in your unworthiness and your belief in your worthiness can seem wide but can be jumped. A young Native American was given this advice at the time of his initiation into the adult community: "As you go the way of life you will see a great chasm. Jump. It is not as wide as you think."

The Temple of Transcendence

Your journey continues but you need rest. Up ahead you notice that the trees thin out and open to a large glen. Inside the glen is a manicured garden, radiant with all varieties of flowers in a wide array of colors. In the center of the garden sits a stone building, ancient and sacred, a place for rest and contemplation. This is the Temple of Transcendence. Within the walls of this temple you will perform an exercise called the Train of Thoughts—designed to help you transcend fear and desire and experience peace. Let us open the door to this great temple.

CHAPTER 7

The Temple of Transcendence

"Have patience with everything
unresolved in your heart
And try to love the questions themselves . . ."

—RAINER MARIA RILKE

—— Finding Peace Together ——

The text message was one word: "Talk?" Tim was pretty sure he knew who it was from, but decided not to respond. If his brother Steve was contacting him it was because he was in trouble again, or needed money. "I'll get back to him in a day or two. Let him cool his heels," Tim thought.

His long history with his troubled brother had worn him down. Once a promising high school and college athlete, Steve's daily life now revolved around his next drug score accompanied by vast quantities of alcohol, all consumed to deaden the pain of a life lost. There was a time, and it seemed a lifetime ago, when all the news from his brother was good news, what great things he was going to be doing in the next new phase of his life. Now, long gone were his high school friends, his future career, and his fiancée—all gone—only he was left, the last person his brother could call for a favor.

The next day Steve's body was found. He had died, not surprisingly, from a toxic combination of pills and alcohol. Authorities had ruled it an accident but ... Tim couldn't shake the idea that he might have prevented Steve's death had he simply answered his brother's text that day.

"It's been five years," Tim said to me. "And I still play 'What if?' over and over in my mind. My family and friends tell me it wasn't my fault, that I had no way of knowing what would have happened. Every time I convince myself they are right, another thought intrudes and casts doubt. It's a perpetual battle inside my head to know the truth. I'm constantly second-guessing myself."

When your life goes into a tailspin, it's common to second-guess yourself. Like Tim, you might feel guilty that you didn't do enough to alter the terrible turn of events, or angry that no one else did, either. Your preoccupation to know specific answers, *why* events played out the way they did in the beginning and *how* they will turn out in the end, creates ever more worry and agitation—the very things you hoped to eliminate. The relentless questions and unrelenting doubts haunt you. You wish to defeat uncertainty—yet you won't experience inner peace by doing battle. The battle is pointless because uncertainty can never be completely defeated. Uncertainty will always be your vexing companion. The highest virtues you seek—love, faith, and hope—do not submit to the lower-self needs for guarantees, deadlines, and neat endings. Yet they're still worth finding because they offer something even better—peace.

Overcoming Fear and Desire

At the entrance to the Temple of Transcendence are two statues, one on each side of the door. On the left is a statue of a child with his hands covering his face. This is Fear. On the right is a statue of a child with her arms extended up. This is Desire. Passing through this entrance and opening the door to the temple, you admit your wish to transcend Fear and Desire.

The ultimate fear of most people is the fear of death, the loss of their life. People also fear psychological death—the loss of their abilities, relationships, reputation, and control over their future. The ultimate wish for most people is to delay death, to gain greater longevity and a greater chance of happiness. Fear and Desire, always within you, inform and assist you in your day-to-day responsibilities, but are also part of your lower self, leading you down the wrong path.

Fear and Desire compel you to try to understand why you suffered pain and loss, why your life is the way it is, and which coping strategies to use. But the coping strategies usually involve fighting, blaming, or withdrawing either into apathy, despair, or addictive habits. Your higher self patiently surrenders to the inevitable disorder of confusion and helplessness that occur when your life is turned upside down. It allows answers to emerge when you are open and ready to receive them. Under stress, your lower self functions primarily in survival mode. When your lower self demands clear-cut answers to the questions *"Why did this happen? How will I go on?"* your higher self says *"Let it be as it is; let it become what it will."* It is within this higher self that a quiet state prevails, that issues become clearer, that intuition expands, that meaningful coincidences are noticed, and that inspired thoughts materialize. It is within this quiet state, when the worries of your mind begin to ebb, that the whisperings of the gods begin to flow.

How do you arrive at your higher state? How do you get past your ego's need to protect you from physical and emotional harm? You tap into your soul's need to experience life fully—in all its sweetness and sorrow. This is how you are transformed.

Joseph Campbell, in his book *Myths to Live By*, asks the question "Who are you between two thoughts?" You identify with your thoughts, they inform you about what you like and don't like, what you believe and don't believe. In the space between two thoughts, what becomes of *you*? Are you simply on standby waiting to get onboard the next train of thoughts that enter your mind? In between two thoughts it is your immortal self that connects you to the deeper meanings of your existence.

In the Temple of Transcendence there is a sacred room, and it is here that you do a special meditation, the Train of Thoughts. This meditation is designed to help you achieve inner peace despite your circumstances. In this room on either side are two eternal flames. One is the flame of Uncertainty—representing those things crucial to your life and happiness of which you have an incomplete understanding or cannot confidently predict. The other is the flame of Mystery—representing those things that remain outside the realm of complete understanding and explanation. You must experience the light and warmth of Uncertainty and Mystery to experience inner peace. Let's examine them now before you do the meditation.

Accept the Mysteries of Life

You have fears you are striving to vanquish and desires you are yearning to fulfill. Such strivings and yearnings, no matter how vital to your safety and growth, create inner tension and conflict. You argue and debate within yourself, trying to figure out the source of your fears, trying to figure out who was to blame for any loss you suffered, and trying to figure out what can be done to help you move forward. Or you argue and debate with others about those things. Here's the mystery: most conflict between two people is really conflict within yourself that is projected outward. We need an enemy without so we don't have to look at the enemy within. The enemy within is all aspects of ourselves we have disowned for fear of seeing ourselves more fully and being open to transformation.

Imagine that there is something you desire but part of you resists that desire for a fearful reason. Imagine that you did something you shouldn't have done and part of you agrees with what you did while the other disagrees. To escape that internal debate, you look outside of yourself and find something or someone to oppose. That way it appears you are taking a clear stand about what you want, how you feel, or what you did, all while making the other person wrong. *"You made me do it!"* or *"You have no right to judge me!"* are internal conflicts projected outward. You made yourself do it. You are judging yourself.

Loss and adversity often cause a person to question his or her worth or the worth of others, the fairness of life, and the meaning of existence. These questions ignite internal debate: *"Am I good? Lovable? Worthwhile? Desirable? Capable? Am I not any of those things?"* The ego, the lower self, is at work there. The ego exists by virtue of dualistic, either/or thinking. It thrives on division. It defines itself by being in opposition to something else. It is narrow-minded. It would rather accept unwise answers that alleviate your fears and help you gain personal desires than to accept wiser answers that challenge you to face your fears and reassess your desires. It seeks certainty, despises doubt. The real problems in your life—those that force you to your knees and shake the foundations of your faith—have no simple solutions. In the big problems of life, you are not aware of, nor do you have control over, all of the variables in play. When calamity strikes, losses accumulate, and pain intensifies, forces seen and unseen play a role in your destiny. You will be powerless to control them all. Sometimes all you can do is sit helplessly and wait it out. Sometimes losses cannot be replaced or pain removed, only accepted.

Accept Uncertainty

As we discussed on the Path of Release, you must accept uncertainty. The Train of Thoughts exercise you'll do shortly allows your opposing thoughts to peacefully coexist with one another, allowing new insights and wisdom to emerge. When you are at peace within, you have no need to project blame onto others and make them your adversaries. This exercise enhances your ability to embrace mystery and uncertainty. This is vital to your emotional and spiritual well-being because the ultimate answers to your most probing questions can never be known with absolute certainty. That leaves you with two choices:

1. You can choose to reduce uncertainty by making life safe and predictable; or
2. You can choose to enter more fully into mystery and uncertainty, willing to experience all that life offers, including sorrow.

When you allow uncertainty and mystery to accompany you on your journey in life, each moment becomes precious because you embrace the reality that change and loss are inevitable. What you have in this moment can vanish in the next.

The Balanced Brain

You might find that you grapple with accepting uncertainties and mysteries on both a practical and an emotional level. That's because of how your brain functions.

Take Tamara, who was in this exact position. Her husband Matt, thirty-nine, had suffered a massive stroke that left the right side of his body paralyzed and took away his ability to speak. Three years later, his condition has improved only slightly. Tamara struggles to remain hopeful. She works a part-time job, bears all of the household responsibilities, and raises their two daughters on her own. Sitting in my office she was clearly depressed, exhausted, and full of worries about the future. "I'm doing everything I used to do and now doing everything Matt used to do. I'm trying to take care of everything and everyone— except myself. How can I go on like this?" she wondered out loud. "Will Matt ever improve so that we can have some of our old life back? How will our situation affect our daughters as they get older?" Slouching forward in her chair with her hands covering her face, she asks: "Is it horrible for me to sometimes think I just want to run away?"

Every serious problem you face affects you on two levels.

1. The first level involves **practical problem-solving**: making decisions about what can be realistically accomplished and how to do it. In Tamara's case, that involves planning her day around the needs of her husband and children. The first level is challenging but it is the second level that knocks the wind out of you.
2. It is in the second level that **worry, anger, despair, and uncertainty** arise when solutions to problems don't fall easily into place or when your life has permanently changed.

You can't obtain inner peace by practical problem-solving efforts alone. Those are short-term fixes. Problems on the second level of one sort or another will always come your way. You obtain inner peace when, in the face of painful challenges, your lower-self fears give way to higher-self wisdom.

Left Brain

Tamara, understandably, wanted inner peace. Yet all her noble efforts were not helping her achieve that. I explained to her that while the left side of her husband's brain was damaged and underfunctioning, the left side of *her* brain was overfunctioning and overengaging in analytical problem-solving. Under stress when the stakes are high, the left brain is motivated by fear. It constantly reviews your situation, digging into the smallest details, looking for answers. Finding no completely satisfying answer, the left brain doubles down, attacking the problem with ever-greater determination. Since problems like Tamara's have no simple solutions, the left brain's efforts only exhausted her, creating greater worry and despair.

Right Brain

The right side of the brain is nonlinear, intuitive, and creative. When you operate out of the right side of your brain, you possess an "I'll go with the flow and cross that bridge when I get there" philosophy. You focus on the big picture, not the small details. The right side of your brain is more activated when you walk:

- the Path of Acceptance and emotionally accept the reality of your situation

- the Path of Inspiration and open yourself to intuitive guidance
- the Path of Release and let go of your desire for control
- the Path of Compassion and look past superficial differences among people

The left side of your brain is more activated when you walk:

- the Path of Resistance and refuse to accept the reality of your circumstances
- the Path of Illusion and block the flow of Divine inspiration
- the Path of Despair and hold on to destructive beliefs
- the Path of Emptiness and fail to use your wisdom for a greater good

Finding Balance

Those who cope well during trying times use the left side of their brains to solve problems that are reasonably solvable, and use the right side of their brains to emotionally accept those things that cannot be easily changed or changed at all. Balancing the left and right sides of the brain will help you achieve calmness and peace. Most people are "left-brain dominant." Under stress they have an automatic tendency to overanalyze the situation in a misguided effort to reduce worry and anxiety by the sheer force of logic. But any positive, hopeful answer they come up with is followed by doubt. *"What if I'm wrong? What if I missed something important? What if things get worse?"* Uncertainty causes overthinking. Overthinking exposes areas of doubt and uncertainty. Uncertainty causes you again to overthink. This becomes a continuous, never-ending loop—an unsuccessful effort to reduce the anxiety created by uncertainty.

When you stop trying to solve problems that cannot be solved and instead adopt a patient "wait and see" attitude, your left brain will put up a fight. It is like a guard dog that barks at people because it thinks it is protecting you, even when those people pose no danger. By practicing the following Train of Thoughts exercise, your brain functions in a more balanced way, creating a greater sense of peace.

Exercise: The Train of Thoughts

When your life is in turmoil, upsetting thoughts roll through your mind, making it impossible for you to feel calm and hopeful. No matter how hard you try to gain a peaceful perspective, the inner debate only adds to your fear and misery.

The Train of Thoughts exercise will change everything. Think of an actual train with a long line of cars attached to the engine as the train emerges very slowly from a tunnel. The train represents the difficult issue you are facing. The tunnel represents your mind. Each car of the train represents one single thought about your situation. You don't need to literally think about a train as you do this exercise. The train is a metaphor to help you notice each separate thought, one at a time, emerge slowly from your mind. These are the steps:

1. Think about what's troubling you the most and rate your overall level of emotional disturbance from zero (none) to ten (extreme).
2. Notice where you feel this general emotional disturbance: stomach, chest, throat, or head.

3. Focus on the issue troubling you and the first thought that emerges. It could be as simple a thought as "I'm so sad" or "I don't think I'll ever get over what has happened" or "I don't know how to handle this."
4. Repeat the same thought prefaced with the words "I accept."
5. Allow your thoughts to continue, one at a time, prefaced by "I accept."
6. Continue until your level of distress has been reduced to zero or one.

As you make each statement, notice whether your subjective level of distress rises, falls, or remains the same. If it rises or remains the same, it means that the statement you just "accepted" still stirs inner conflict. You need to continue to express more thoughts about the issue. If you say *"I accept that I'm so unhappy"* and then notice that your level of distress rises, you probably have a host of other thoughts such as *"But I don't want to be unhappy"* or *"It's not fair what happened to me"* or *"I'm scared I'll never be happy again . . . ."* Each of those statements also needs to be restated with the words "I accept."

There is one other important rule to follow. Anytime you ask yourself a question, rephrase it into a statement. *"What if the worst happens?"* becomes *"I'm frightened that the worst will happen."*

Then repeat the statement with the words "I accept." *"I accept that I'm frightened that the worst will happen."* Peace is not achieved by asking worrisome questions. It is achieved by managing your lower-self fears and desires by using higher-self values.

When you preface each thought with the words "I accept" you balance the hemispheres of your brain. The right side of your brain says "I accept" while the left side of your brain offers additional commentary. It is important to say "I accept" even if two successive thoughts are completely contradictory. For example, your typical, uncorrected train of thought may go something like this:

How can I ever forgive him for cheating on me?
But I want to forgive him . . .
I just don't know how to forgive . . .
It's not fair . . .
I don't deserve this . . .
But I still love him . . .
How can I ever trust him again?
But I want him in my life . . .

Rephrased, that train of thought would go like this:

I accept that I'm worried I can never forgive him for cheating on me.
I accept that I want to forgive him.
I accept that I don't know how to forgive.
I accept that it's not fair.
I accept that I don't deserve this.
I accept that I still love him.
I accept that I'm worried that I may be unable to trust him.
I accept that I want him in my life.

When you accept even a negative, self-critical thought such as *"I am worthless,"* you are not accepting the validity of that thought, but only the fact that such a thought exists right now in your mind. The common tendency is to challenge a negative thought, but that creates resistance and resistance undermines inner peace. You will discover that by accepting all of your thoughts—the positive and the negative, the rational and the irrational—the thoughts that create tension will drop away on their own. You won't have to force them.

When you "accept" each and every thought—no matter how irrational or negative—you halt the internal debate that would otherwise add to your stress and frustration. Acceptance keeps you from running in circles. There is a principle in neuroscience known as Hebb's Law, which states that the thought patterns you use when trying to manage your stress create neural pathways that become more entrenched the more you use them. Your back-and-forth debates and never-ending "What if's?" become so habitual, so mindless, that you hardly notice when you engage in them. When you repeat the words "I accept" in front of each and every thought, you begin to develop new neural pathways in the right side of your brain. It is only by gaining greater access to the right side of your brain that you will develop true inner peace.

You should do the Train of Thoughts exercise daily. It can take a few minutes to perhaps twenty minutes depending upon how many thoughts you have. If you have limited time, a short version can help. Anytime you are troubled—even by a small event, a spilled drink or heavy traffic—simply say *"I accept my situation as it is even if I don't like it. And I have faith and trust that things will work out as well as can reasonably be expected."* The more you practice this thinking, the more you will transcend your lower-self fears and desires and the more peace you will feel.

A Variation on This Exercise

You cultivate inner peace when you seek a higher, nobler level of conscious awareness and stop trying to control situations where you really don't actually have control. Each of the four Paths of Transformation taps into one of those higher levels. Tolerance, faith, trust, and love represent the core aspects of the Paths of Acceptance, Inspiration, Release, and Compassion. The Train of Thoughts exercise begins with acceptance, but any noble virtue could be used in the exercise. You might say *"I accept my situation with faith, trust, and love."* A negative statement can also be accepted with faith, trust, and love such as *"I accept with faith, trust, and love that right now I feel hopeless."* Higher-level virtues move a person toward peace, even when the initial train of thoughts is negative or despairing.

Overcoming Your Left Brain's Obstacles

The Train of Thoughts exercise is different from popular advice to simply "think positive." Positive thoughts are important, yes. They can increase your optimism and motivate you to persevere when the going gets rough. But when fear takes over, positive thoughts are countered by negative thoughts, forcing inner debates and conflicts. Peace is gained by letting go of the inner battle altogether, by accepting each thought as it emerges from your mind without judging or opposing it. If an opposing thought naturally follows, it too is accepted without any concern for the obvious contradiction. This is especially important when your losses are permanent or solutions to your problems remain distant and uncertain. This exercise steers you away from attempts to find answers to things you cannot control. It allows you to detach yourself from outcomes, from destinations, and instead focus on your journey. It allows you to be open to insights and intuitions that are only accessible in a calm, uncluttered, trusting state of mind.

Once you begin the Train of Thoughts exercise, your left brain will try to thwart your success. Under stress your left brain agitates you, demanding that you find answers to your worries. It seduces you into thinking that unless you come up with remedies or action-plans for your problems, inner peace is impossible. But the reverse is true. Until you generate some degree of inner peace, you may be unable to manage your problems. The left brain is where your ego resides. The more control your ego has, the more you find yourself saying "I do *not* accept things as they are. I do *not* accept guidance with which I don't agree. I do *not* accept what I do not fully understand or trust."

Following are the common thoughts that pull you into left-brain thinking, and the corresponding statements that move you back into right-brain thinking:

LEFT-BRAIN THOUGHT	RIGHT-BRAIN THOUGHT
But I *don't* accept this!	*I accept that I don't accept this.*
I *don't* want to work this exercise!	*I accept that I don't want to work this exercise.*
I *don't* want to do this!	*I accept that I don't want to do this.*
I *can't* live with uncertainty!	*I accept that I can't live with uncertainty.*
I *need* to know what will happen!	*I accept that I need to know what will happen.*
If I trust I am likely to get hurt!	*I accept that if I trust I am likely to get hurt.*
I *don't* want to accept a negative thought!	*I accept that I don't want to accept a negative thought.*

Simply by prefacing those thoughts with the phrase "I accept," you move back into right-brain awareness. When you accept each and every successive thought, no matter how negative, irrational, or contradictory, your train of thoughts keeps moving you forward toward a peaceful destination. Eventually, even the most negative thought gets followed by a more optimistic one. For example, the thought *"I can't live with uncertainty"* will at some point lead to a thought such as *"But I will try"* or *"Maybe I can learn to live with uncertainty."* Once reassuring thoughts are accepted, calmness comes. That reduction in tension will continue until your next worry comes along, as it will. Then your tension will once again rise and, ultimately, dissipate when you have accepted all of your competing thoughts about that area of concern. Amazingly, you will discover that you feel more peaceful even when you have not come up with any solutions. If there is something you could do that you have overlooked, peacefully accepting all thoughts will allow that insight to emerge naturally.

The Tower in the Temple

In the Temple of Transcendence, there is a staircase leading up to the top of a tower and into a large, airy chamber. This chamber, surrounded by windows, lets you look out to the horizon in all directions. Here you have the opportunity to examine your core beliefs and perhaps modify your perspective on life. This is your opportunity to understand how paradox and mystery, rather than being obstacles to experiencing wisdom and peace, are doorways.

CHAPTER 8

The Chamber of Perspective

"Who looks outside, sleeps;
Who looks inside, awakens."

—CARL JUNG

—— Finding Peace Together ——

Peter repeatedly assured his mother that the pending surgery was "Just routine. Nothing bad will happen." He had indeed entered the hospital for minor surgery but something went horribly wrong. The worst happened, a serious medical error, and Peter never regained consciousness. He was placed in a rehabilitation center where he lay in a comatose state. His mother would visit him there nearly every day.

"I always talk to him, hoping he hears me," Rose told me. Everyone knew that Rose was a devout Christian and knew she had lived her life trying to be a good person. She believed that her unflinching devotion to her religion would one day reward her. She believed that in time her son would wake up completely healed. When the call came from the rehabilitation center, Rose could scarcely believe what she was hearing. Peter had suddenly passed away. Rose felt betrayed by everyone: the doctors who operated on Peter, the medical personnel at the rehab center—but mostly by God.

"People tell me everything happens for a reason. What reason? Can *you* tell me the reason God would allow this to happen to my son?"

"I don't know the reason," I said. "And frankly, if someone told me 'Everything happens for a reason' immediately after a person I dearly loved had died, I'd feel like slugging him."

"I feel the same way," she said. "But there must be an answer. There must be . . ."

In times of great loss, many of our assumptions about life are shattered. The values we hold dear can seemingly abandon us and we are left without a true moral compass. Clichés offered, such as *"It was God's will—There's a season for everything—It was his time to go—God only gives you what you can handle—At least her suffering has ended—"* often hurt more than they help.

Outgrowing Your Old Beliefs to Build a New Future

Statements like these hurt because you are being told "Don't think and feel the way you do" and you are lonelier for it. There is a time and place for well-meaning advice, but most of us need some passage of time before we are open to receiving it. In profound grief, you work through your pain by undertaking a transformational journey; simple advice might offer momentary comfort but it cannot exempt you from your journey. Your journey is part of your destiny.

There are two situations when you are most open to new perspectives on how to cope with your losses and hardships.

1. The first is when you feel that the advice-giver has a heartfelt understanding of your situation and, instead of trying to talk you out of your pain, lets you know it makes sense. When you feel you are deeply understood, you are willing to hear—and perhaps heed—the advice.

2. The second is when events have so battered you, when you feel so abandoned, when your strengths no longer sustain you, when despair and disillusionment settle in and you are so convinced you have nothing left to lose, that you finally surrender. That is when you open yourself to see your world through different eyes. Your surrender represents a kind of psychological and spiritual death. But in every sacred tradition—and in nature itself—rebirth always follows death.

In the epic journeys told in classic stories and myths, the hero returns home where the story began, once upon a time. The hero has been transformed and now looks at life from a new vantage point. In the Chamber of Perspective you can formulate a new, meaningful view of the events of your life. During a transformation, you either expand your former beliefs and see layers and deeper meanings you never saw before, or you release those beliefs entirely. All beliefs, true or false, help you to structure your current life. You then know what to expect and how to interpret the meaning of events. Beliefs reveal vistas you've yet to explore if you are willing to tap into the origins and implications of those beliefs. But they can simultaneously limit vistas by building a high fence.

Then something happens to shake those beliefs. It could be something uplifting: the birth of a child, the birth of a loving relationship, or the birth of a dream-come-true. It could be something dispiriting: the death of what had once been vital to your happiness. Then the old fence barriers fall away. You realize that some of the beliefs that once limited you now open your eyes to new horizons, and some beliefs that once guided you now leave you blind. This can be a confusing time on your journey when your internal compass now points to true north but in a direction other than what you always believed. The wise person understands that the old ideas—even if they are now abandoned—taught lessons, and all lessons learned are part of one's life path and worthy of gratitude.

The New View

If you are to begin your transformation, your journey must force you to re-examine some of your beliefs. Transformation starts to occur when your beliefs come in conflict with reality. That is when something must give. But the outcome—what you finally believe—is less important than your willingness to struggle with the confusion and contradictions that underlie any belief system. Some of the greatest spiritual teachings, such as "God is love," sound simple. But anyone who has suffered a tragic loss will tell you that God's loving ways sometimes seem unloving. The closer one gets to an understanding of God, the more one discovers paradox and mystery.

When beliefs come in conflict with reality, you have three choices:

1. Redefine beliefs.
2. Redefine reality.
3. Look for deeper meanings that embrace both your beliefs and reality.

Suppose you are walking on a street and the person in front of you reaches into his pocket for his gloves, and a twenty-dollar bill accidentally flutters out of his pocket and falls to the ground. You decide to pick it up and keep it. If you regard yourself as an honest person, that act now creates internal conflict. A remedy for that conflict would be to change your view of yourself and conclude that you are not so honest after all. More likely, you might make excuses and tell yourself that you really need the money and the other person probably does not—thereby maintaining your view of yourself as a fairly honest, albeit needy, person. Or you might alter reality. You might try to convince yourself that it was really someone else who had dropped the money earlier. Each of those cases offers a quick remedy with little struggle—and with no transformation, either. For transformation to occur, you need to look inward and grapple with what just happened. You might then awaken to the idea that you have been dishonest many times in the past without ever having realized it. What would you then do with that new self-awareness? Or you might examine why your desire for free money overcame the nobler goal of being an honest person. Or you might explore why you felt entitled to keep money that isn't yours because someone was a bit careless. Unless you grapple with those and other related questions, you will not transform.

Embrace the Paradoxes All Around You

It is common to have a dream for your life and endeavor to make it come true. But sometimes, when everything has fallen beautifully into place, something happens to alter the direction of your life in ways you never planned. The late actor Christopher Reeve, famous for his role in the *Superman* movies, had his world upended when he suffered a spinal cord injury that made him a quadriplegic. Yet he and his wife Dana became an inspiration to millions—not only in their devotion to one another—but in their devotion to calling attention to the plight of others with spinal cord injuries. Before his death in 2004, he started the Christopher Reeve Foundation to raise money for spinal cord research and to improve the life of people with disabilities. Today he is remembered for his courage and humanitarianism.

It is only when your life stops making sense that it can start to make sense. That is a paradox that contains truth. But if a truth contradicts itself, how can it be true? As you travel on your transformational journey, you will come face to face with the ultimate questions of your existence: *Who am I? Why was I born at a certain time and place in history? Why do I exist at all? Do I exist after death? Does God guide me? Does God even exist?* Those questions lead you to paradox. Mystics tell us that only in paradox can one begin to comprehend the incomprehensible—itself a paradoxical statement. Paradox unsettles your rational mind and creates agitation that is necessary for inner growth and—paradoxically—for inner stability. The more comfortable you are in your beliefs, the less likely you will be to ever look beyond them, ever probe more deeply into them, or ever grasp their truest meanings. It is the rare person who plumbs the full depths of their cherished beliefs. Typically, we examine our beliefs just enough until we feel comfortable with them and deem them both correct and useful. Such beliefs may offer consolation in troubled times but sometimes a harsh reality clashes with those beliefs forcing a re-examination. Paradox forces you to admit that all you really know for sure is that you don't know for sure. It compels you to reach beyond the comfort and convenience of established beliefs and either seek a fuller understanding of them or change them entirely. Paradox compels you to embrace ideas that appear to be logically impossible but that tap into deeper, more profound truths. Most important of all, paradox takes you from either/or thinking into unified thinking. Remember, Niels Bohr, the brilliant twentieth-century physicist, said, "The opposite of a great truth is another great truth."

A paradoxical idea is not a byproduct of word play but a genuine part of the material (real) world and at the heart of the immaterial (spiritual) world. Scientists like Niels Bohr have long surrendered to paradoxes and contradictions. A single photon of light—a tiny dot, a particle—exists *simultaneously* as a long wave. Information between subatomic particles can be transmitted in zero-time—faster than the speed of light—which is mathematically impossible. There is debate among physicists about whether the universe is infinitely large or simply finite, but physicists agree that the universe is expanding. What is it expanding *into*? Is there something outside of the universe that is not part of the universe? In mathematics, some formulas that accurately define real physical states must use the square root of minus-one—an *imaginary number*—to make the equation work. Paradox is woven into the fabric of reality and perhaps even defines reality. And yet when we question why tragedies and misfortune happen, why some people die so young, or why a loving and all-powerful God allows horrific suffering, we expect the answers to be flawlessly logical.

Paradox may be your vexing companion, but—surprisingly—it is also a friend. It allows you to stretch your curiosity, to peek behind the awe-inspiring or the horrifying to glimpse the mysterious. That glimpse shapes your new perspective. New perspective brings greater understanding. Paradoxically, greater understanding leads to more questions—which make you realize that you now understand even less.

Exercise: Consider Seven Paradoxical Ideas

I hope that the seven paradoxical ideas listed in this section will make you curious. Explore their implications for your life and your current journey. The ideas are not necessarily true—or false. They are meant simply to inspire you to consider things you might not have considered before from a unique angle—or to consider more fully the things you have given only scant reflection. As you contemplate new possibilities, you're helping yourself build a peaceful future beyond your loss.

I chose the number seven because that number has sacred meaning in religious traditions. For example, in Islam there are seven levels of heaven. In Buddhism, there are seven factors of enlightenment. In Judaism, the Menorah has seven branches and seven represents wholeness and completeness. In the early Christian tradition, there were seven sacraments, which have been maintained currently by Roman Catholicism and certain other Christian faiths. Each sacrament represents a rite of passage to a new phase of one's spiritual life. Whether or not you adhere to a Christian faith, the sacraments also represent aspects of the heroic journey that everyone takes regardless of religion. The sacraments relate to the Eastern (Hindu) concept of the seven chakras, explained brilliantly by Caroline Myss in her book *Anatomy of the Spirit*.

The seven sacraments and what they represent in terms of emotional and spiritual development are:

1. Baptism: Your world into which you are born; accepting your culture, family, and traditions.
2. Communion: Your need to relate to others; developing meaningful relationships.
3. Confirmation: Your initiation into adulthood; developing the skills of a warrior.
4. Marriage: Your loving devotion to another; uniting for something greater than yourself.
5. Penance: Your responsibility for your choices; being unwilling to blame others.
6. Ordination: Your seeking of what is sacred; seeing beyond what is ordinary.
7. Last Rites: Your preparation for death; returning to your true home.

The seven paradoxical statements are parallel to the seven sacraments and the seven chakras:

1. You are unique, everything is one. (Baptism; the root chakra)
2. You despise in others what you accept in yourself. (Communion; the sacral chakra)
3. You fulfill the purpose of death when you live fully. (Confirmation; the solar plexus chakra)
4. You change when you become who you are already. (Marriage; the heart chakra)

5. You create your destiny by your choices, realizing that some destiny is fate. (Penance; the throat chakra)
6. You see most clearly when in darkness. (Ordination; the third-eye chakra)
7. You are ordinary, you are mystical. (Last Rites; the crown chakra)

Let's take a closer look at each paradox.

1. You Are Unique; Everything Is One

You start out as a member of a family or community and that is where your initial identity lies. Some of the more difficult choices you make in life may involve challenging and possibly opposing family values or rules or the traditions of your community or culture. Any choice that clashes with your group's expectations or with any organization to which you belong can create guilt and tension. Once you have been initiated into a group—whether birth, vocation, or dues—you may be expected to believe in certain principles, to vote a certain way, to not upset any organizational apple carts. Every group or family provides stability, but stability prevents change.

A friend of mine has had a strained relationship with his father for decades. His dad raised him to be an atheist but my friend believes in God. When a politician votes his or her conscience and goes against the party's wishes, colleagues will judge that politician harshly. Pressure to conform to group standards causes many people to forgo their own sense of right and wrong. Conflict comes when you wish to evolve away from the group. Organizations tend to evolve slowly; families evolve a bit faster.

The more completely you identify with a particular group, the more likely you are to evolve at the rate of that particular group. The more radical a personal change you make—convert to a different religion, leave the family business, change your politics or your gender—the less likely your family or group will be to cheer you on. It takes an enlightened person to not feel threatened by you when you hold a very different view of how life should be lived.

Sometimes your own inner urgings coax you to leave the family circle and create your own unique way of life. Other times something dramatic and unexpected happens that forces you to rethink everything you once thought was true. That is when you come face to face with your fears. If you give in to fear, you will not change. If you face your fears, you will change but you will necessarily release something important to you—a belief system, a relationship, a habit, or a way of life.

You *are* unique. And your soul yearns to expand. For that to occur, you must, in some way, separate yourself from others. And yet the belief "We are one" remains a universal, sacred concept. Perhaps the paradox is best understood by realizing that only at your highest level of consciousness is the belief "We are all one" fully experienced. But to attain that highest level you must be willing to "leave home." Once transformed, you return home. But like Dorothy in *The Wizard of Oz*, wishing to return to Kansas, or a soldier wanting to leave the battlefield, home has a different feel now because your perspective has changed. It is home, and yet it isn't. Once your perspective changes, you can never go back to what it once was. Thomas Wolfe was right when he said, "You can't go home again."

2. You Despise in Others What You Accept in Yourself

You are capable of much greater good than you know, and also greater evil. Most people don't like to look at this "shadow" side. One clue to your shadow side is to pay attention to what you despise in others. You might think it despicable to kill someone in cold blood. You may claim that you would never do such a thing. Most likely you wouldn't. But every week someone comes into my office and tells me they did something they never imagined they would do. Even if you are sure you would never commit a certain act, you probably have already done so in a symbolic way. You, of course, may never have committed murder, never actually killed someone, but have you ever "killed" someone's spirit by cruelly mocking or insulting them? Have you ever "killed" someone's dream by ridiculing it? You may not have stolen money from someone, but have you ever "stolen" his or her reputation with malicious gossip? Maybe you wouldn't tell lies, but do you lie to yourself about your true nature and what is in your best interest?

When you glimpse anything about yourself that makes you uncomfortable, do you turn away? If so, you will readily see in others what you try to hide from yourself. You cannot control something by suppressing it. Suppression ultimately leads to a backlash. It is only when you can accept your dark side that you bring it into the light.

The second chakra (the sacrament of Communion) pertains to your need to develop meaningful relationships and to recognize that everyone has a Divine purpose. First you are welcomed into a family or group (first chakra and the sacrament of Baptism), then you learn to commune with others, to get along. It is here you develop the power to create and the power to control. If you overdo those powers—if they become ends in themselves rather than means to more noble ends—your shadow side has taken over. Inevitably, something dramatic will happen to you as it does to everyone—a loss, a calamity, or an upheaval—that begins your transformational journey. If your shadow side is in charge, you will resist walking the Four Paths of Transformation and your journey will be harder. Your higher self is willing to let go of whatever holds you back. Your lower self insists on retaining power at all costs.

3. You Fulfill the Purpose of Death When You Live Fully

In the opening of any movie or dramatic story, the ordinary day-to-day happenings of life are always interrupted by an "event"—something exciting that goes wrong or something unexpected that sets the story in motion. On your transformational journey, that event was some major loss that sent you reeling. In terms of sacraments and chakras, the adolescent is expected to fight and be willing to die for nobler principles and beliefs.

Death is instructive. It teaches you that life as you now know it will end one day, so living your life to its fullest becomes more imperative. I've worked with a number of clients in the prime of their life who were physically healthy but intensely afraid of dying. Fearing death, they also feared life. I've also worked with people with terminal illnesses who were not afraid of dying as much as they feared missing out on the fullness of whatever their lives still had to offer. For them, the smallest thing—the sound of the wind through the trees—could generate an inner glow, a sense of the sublime. When I work with people who fear driving across bridges, it is not unusual for them to also fear the transitions of life that bridges symbolically represent. They may fear leaving home, getting married or getting divorced, changing careers, or pursuing a dream. They fear panic attacks while on the bridge, of feeling trapped and losing emotional control, but they have actually taken too harsh a control over their lives in order to avoid facing fears and have trapped themselves. Proclaiming a hearty "Yes!" to life means you must also heartily proclaim "Yes!" to your inevitable death. Death is part of life and happens in small ways every day.

The third chakra represents your relationship to yourself and your degree of self-knowledge as you face life's challenges. On the transformational journey you will deal with problems you can't manage using your current self-awareness, skills, and beliefs. It is on the Path of Release that you begin to set aside old beliefs that no longer serve you. That release is a kind of death, but a necessary occurrence so that you can live more fully in spite of your losses.

4. You Change When You Become Who You Are Already

There is the story of a sculptor, possibly Michelangelo, who, when asked how he was able to carve such a beautiful horse out of a block of marble, replied, "I simply cut away everything that isn't a horse." The message: You already have access to what you need in order to persevere on your journey. You don't have to *add to* who you are, but rather *let go of* who you are not.

In challenging situations, some people "rise to the occasion," which is to say they have abandoned their fear and discovered an inner strength they didn't know they possessed. As in the state of marriage where "two become one," this stage of your journey is revealed along the Path of Inspiration where there is a greater connection to Divine energy, and the Path of Compassion where you sacrifice yourself for others. The heart's true love is not about money, possessions, or self-gratification; it is about the greatest good.

In the chakra system, the heart chakra represents the love that resides within and is your true power source. It's the dividing line between the physical self and the spiritual self; between the lower self's demands for control and the higher self's willingness to "let go and let God." In marriage, you bridge your lower-self needs for safety, security, and companionship with higher-self values of love, trust, forgiveness, and the union of souls.

The inspired heart can see life's beauty through a veil of tears. It recognizes that your cry of grief is also your song of love. It understands that your heartbreak gives birth to heart-wisdom. Whereas the mind is a dispassionate observer to love that cannot fully define the experience, your heart, where love resides, is a passionate participant.

You may not have considered this before, but it is also within your nature to be a healing presence. Whenever you let go of judgments about how other people's situations should be, whenever you accept "what is," you rise above the demands of your righteous ego and engage your higher self. Your presence has healing properties by allowing others to simply "be." They can breathe easier and express their opinions more honestly. The seeds of healing will take root; they will not be judged but heard, not corrected but understood, not rejected but accepted. In the book *The Healing Brain*, James Lynch reports that no disease is more deadly than loneliness. Mortality rates are more accurately predicted not by the habits of smoking or exercise but by the abundance or lack of social connections people have in their lives. People with more social connections live longer, period. You have an opportunity every day, with every interaction, to radiate warmth and healing.

5. You Create Your Destiny by Your Choices, But Some Destiny Is Fate

On a cold January night in 1973, I was seventeen years old, had had my driver's license for two months, and was driving down a hill covered in a sheet of black ice. I lost control of the car and it spun in a complete circle as it skidded down the hill, stopping only when the rear of the car hit a tree. Amazingly, I was not injured, and as anyone who has been a teenager will tell you, the experience was upsetting but not traumatic. I gave it no more thought in the decades after. Six years ago, while sitting with clients throughout the day, the memory of that accident intruded on my mind for no obvious reason. Finally I realized that the date happened to be January twenty-second and I assumed that my subconscious mind had remembered the anniversary. The next day the memory returned but with greater force, playing itself out like a silent movie. On the morning of the third day I could hear in my mind the crunch of the car as it hit the tree. The entire memory intensified in the next several hours.

Finally, in the middle of the afternoon my cell phone rang. The caller ID said it was my daughter but when I said hello the voice on the other end belonged to a state trooper. He assured me that my daughter was fine but she'd been driving down a steep hill and hit black ice, and her car spun completely in a circle before finally coming to a stop when the rear of her car hit a tree. My daughter was seventeen. She'd had her driver's license for two months. She had the exact same accident I'd had decades earlier—almost to the day. Clearly, I'd had a premonition. Did that mean my daughter's car accident was preordained? Despite all of the choices she made that day while driving, was fate involved in her accident?

The fifth chakra deals with willpower and the choices you make. The sacrament of Penance involves taking responsibility for your choices. The choices you make create your destiny but so do random events, with luck and happenstance playing a role. If some things are preordained to happen regardless of what you do, then the mystery of forces unseen also plays a role. As you examine each of the sacraments, the chakras, and the steps along your journey, you will notice that your progress moves from dependence and vulnerability to the development of personal power and ultimately to the relinquishing of much of your control to a higher source of good. The Path of Inspiration allows you to become aware of guidance coming from unseen sources, such as the guidance that you get from meaningful coincidences, intuition, and inspired wisdom. But to heed that guidance you must be willing to align your will with the will of the Source—not always an easy task.

Here is a simple exercise that will help you fine-tune your intuition. Say out loud "My name is … " and then state your name. Notice how it feels to truthfully state your name. Next, say "My name is … " but make up a false name. Notice how it feels to state something you know to be untrue. That subtle difference in feeling represents your body's way of telling you yes or no. If you have to make a decision and you are unsure what to do, notice the subtle way your body responds when you tell yourself you will act first in one way then another. Notice the decision with which your body agrees.

Mary was a recent college graduate who wanted to return to school to become either a nurse or a speech therapist. Raised in a family with a strict religious code, she always feared doing anything that would be considered wrong. As a result, she hesitated when making important decisions. Now that she couldn't make up her own mind on her career, she tried unsuccessfully to discern what God would want her to do. When she did the previous exercise she realized that she preferred to be a speech therapist. "But is that God's will?" she asked me. I told her I did not know God's will for her. I had a hard enough time figuring out what is God's will for me. Mary's real problem was that she never developed a strong sense of personal power. She went from trying to do what her parents thought was right to trying to do what God thought was right and never figured out what *she* thought was right. Surrendering one's will to God's will happens at a high level of spiritual development. But a person must first understand her own will before it can be surrendered. That means undertaking your own struggle with life's ups and downs and learning from your mistakes.

6. You See Most Clearly When in Darkness

The sacrament of Ordination corresponds to the third-eye chakra, according to author Caroline Myss. Although in Christian religions Ordination is a sacrament for those wishing to enter a ministry, this sacrament can generally symbolize the higher calling meant for everyone. The third-eye chakra also represents the ability to see what others do not; to look further and deeper within the landscape of our hearts, minds, and souls to gain a new perspective.

Joe was able to do that after a heartbreaking loss. His wife and three-year-old son had both died in a terrible car accident. Bereft for several years, Joe finally met and married Candace. He now has an eight-year-old son, Timothy.

"I loved my first wife and son with all my heart. But now I can't imagine life without Candace and Tim. Tim wouldn't even be alive had my first wife and son not died. I decided long ago to stop trying to figure out why things happen the way they do. I accept my situation and try to make the best of it."

Joe realized years ago that if he maintained a dualistic way of seeing things—right or wrong, good or bad—he would never be happy. If he could go back to his past life, would he? If he did, then he would lose Candace and Tim, the two people he now cherishes most in the world. But having them in his life was a consequence of losing two other people he cherished. How can he feel grateful for his new family when the price for that family was paid by the death of his first wife and child? In the darkness of his grief, he saw the light of a bigger truth: Love, acceptance, gratitude, and forgiveness are the only way out of the pain and confusion of adversity.

"I believe that things happen *for* us, not *to* us," Joe said. I don't try to figure out the reason. Sometimes I get a glimpse of what I think is the reason but I'm never really sure."

The darkness in life is part of the wholeness of life. If you tread too carefully through life, avoiding all that might be hurtful or wrong, you will live not humbly but superficially. You will never plumb the depths of your human nature. You will be running from something but never learn exactly what it is. Your goal is not to purposely set out to do hurtful things—but given your humanness you will do them anyway. Your goal is to examine the deeper meanings of why you do what you do, what fears and desires lay hidden in your heart. The dark side of your heart sheds light on your soul.

7. You Are Ordinary, You Are Mystical

I was in high school when I met Father Bob Arpin. He was a newly ordained priest and chaplain at Smith College in my hometown of Northampton, Massachusetts. Shy, short in stature, and quite overweight, he possessed a remarkable quality, a beautiful singing voice. We would hear him sing at Mass on Sundays.

One day when classes at St. Michael's High School ended, my friends and I rushed to leave the building. As Father Bob passed us in the hallway, he asked if we could spare some time to help him pack some boxes and move them into his car. Before I could speak, my friends responded with a quick and firm "No." We had places to go, things to do.

As my friends ran off I stood there, hesitant. I wanted to help but . . . "Paul, come on!" I heard my friends call. I knew that despite our plans we had time to give Father Bob a hand. But the pressure to fit in with the crowd—and to avoid what I knew would be their teasing had I stayed behind to help—was stronger than doing the right thing. "Sorry, Father," I said. "I gotta go."

Even as I joined my friends, I regretted my actions. It was a clear moment for me, a time when I became painfully aware that some of my values needed an upgrade. That day I fell short of taking a stand, but this shy priest went on to take a courageous and very public stand. And even though I did not help him store some boxes when I was young, now that I'm older I'd like to take his tale out of storage, for it is inspiring and worth telling.

In 1987, two months after learning of his illness, Father Bob Arpin became the first Catholic priest to admit publicly that he was gay—and gravely ill from AIDS. In the 1980s, such an admission was scandalous. Father Bob appeared as a guest on several national talk shows and quickly garnered worldwide recognition.

In his book, *Wonderfully, Fearfully Made*, published before he died in 1995 at the age of forty-eight, Father Bob wrote how as a child and young seminarian he'd been the brunt of cruel jokes for being very overweight. "For as long as I can remember I've been fat," he wrote. His public admission about his sexuality and illness opened him up to even more public ridicule and, worse, contempt.

Once he received a letter from a woman claiming to be a nun. She told him that he was an abomination to God and she hoped he would die from AIDS. Father Bob's response was, "Along with the awareness that I was sick and dying came the sense that I had nothing to lose. For the first time in my life I was free to say and be who I am without being afraid . . . And like every gift I've received from God it is a call to ministry, a call to use my life to proclaim the good news that God loves us just as we are."

After retiring from his ministerial duties for medical reasons, Father Bob nonetheless worked tirelessly in his remaining years to help comfort AIDS patients and their families, raise money for charities like the United Way, and educate students, teachers, and members of the clergy of all religions on AIDS awareness. He ran support groups, visited the dying, and offered encouragement and comfort to clergy members of all faiths who felt abandoned because of their sexual orientation, and anyone who felt too frightened to publicly admit that they, too, had AIDS. Father Bob rose above ridicule and with a humble heart achieved what is noble and maybe even holy. Though an "ordinary" person, his influence was indeed extraordinary—even mystical. And it was paradoxical that after having retired from the priesthood, Father Bob lived a life that represented the highest virtues of a priest.

When I gaze upon beautiful things in nature—a vast ocean, a majestic waterfall, a serene sunset, a snow-draped forest—I see the close union of artistry and mysticism. Breathtaking beauty is mystical. What is mystical—seemingly profound and difficult to grasp—is actually ordinary, commonplace, there for all to see. I call it God's poetry. All things start small: "Mighty oaks from little acorns grow." Even the universe with its trillions of stars began infinitely small before the Big Bang. God's poetry also reveals itself in more modest ways when people from humble beginnings achieve greatness. Imagine our own American history without the humble beginnings and humble hearts of our greatest presidents, George Washington and Abraham Lincoln.

The crown chakra coincides with the Christian sacrament of the Last Rites. It represents the place on your journey where physical concerns give way to spiritual awareness and fear gives way to peace.

Peace is found not because you have fixed all that is broken, from broken hearts to broken relationships, or answered all manner of questions on the meaning of life. Peace comes from fully accepting all the moments of your life, the good and the bad, the honorable and the dishonorable, the sacred and the profane. Peace comes from forgiveness. It is a rare person who, on their deathbed, has tied up all the loose ends of his or her life. The last option at the end of life for inner peace is acceptance, forgiveness, and perhaps a hope for something more beyond what is known.

The closer you get to this highest spiritual calling, the more likely that you will fall, at least temporarily, into a spiritual abyss. C.S. Lewis, the Christian scholar and author of the *Narnia* books, wrote passionately about the power of prayer and the role of suffering in forging a strong spiritual life. Yet when his beloved wife died of cancer, he experienced a feeling of deep desolation, a "dark night of the soul." In Christianity, the "dark night of the soul" is a common rite of passage to know the Divine. C.S. Lewis thought he had the answers to many of the most puzzling theological questions. Yet in his book *A Grief Observed*, he writes how the God he had befriended seemed eerily silent during the period of his most intense grief. "When I lay these questions before God I get no answer. But a rather special sort of 'No answer.' It is not the locked door. It is more like a silent, certainly not uncompassionate, gaze. As though He shook his head not in refusal but waiving the question. Like, 'Peace, child; you don't understand.'"

The Illumination

It is time now to leave the temple and continue your journey. Up ahead is a high hill. You gaze at its topmost point and see small circles of light, what seem like flames that glow bright but do not burn. As you climb this hill you see more clearly. The circles of light are people, like you, who have been illuminated by their journey. From this perspective they can see off in the distance to the place where their journey began, the winding roads and paths, the high hills and mountains they have traveled, and from where they've gained wisdom.

As you reach the hilltop and join those who have arrived before you, you too will be illuminated.

Indeed, you are now.

CHAPTER 9

The Illumination

"Those who think they know how the
universe could have been had they created it—
without pain, without sorrow, without time,
without death—are unfit for illumination."

—JOSEPH CAMPBELL

—— Finding Peace Together ——

Mattie was just a toddler. The tracheal tube in his throat made it
hard for him to speak but, bright boy that he was, he'd learned
American Sign Language to help him communicate. He and
his brother, Jamie, older by a year, both suffered from a rare
form of muscular dystrophy. Jamie had lost all meaningful vision
two years earlier. Still, Mattie, who couldn't easily speak, had
used sign language to "read" stories to his beloved older brother.
Jamie would smile anyway despite his loss of vision, and Mattie
communicated anyway because he wanted to make his older
brother happy. After the death of his older brother, Mattie would
want his mother to remind him again and again how he and his
brother found ways to care for each other.

Mattie Stepanek was a remarkable boy who passed away in 2004 just before his fourteenth birthday. His favorite color was sunrise. His second favorite was rainbow. At age five he spoke about "heartsongs"—his word to describe the deeper purpose of one's life, "our sense of why we are here and how we can keep going." He wrote poems that spoke of pain and loss but were mostly about hope, love, and—most important of all—peace.

In her beautiful book *Messenger: The Legacy of Mattie J.T. Stepanek*, Mattie's mother Jeni writes eloquently about Mattie and his sister and brothers. Jeni Stepanek was diagnosed with that same form of muscular dystrophy as an adult. She was told that the disease was not hereditary. But the fact remained that all four of her children eventually succumbed to the illness; Mattie never met his older sister Katie or brother Stevie, who died before he was born.

Mattie had a joy for living despite the severe challenges he faced. He had wisdom far beyond his years. He was determined to live life fully, "However you press me, and pain me, and dare me . . . I shall find peace in the storm of disease. I shall find joy in the heart of pain . . . I shall be an ambassador of love." Mattie went on to write *Heartsongs*, the first of his seven *New York Times* bestselling books. He hoped to be remembered as a "poet, a peacemaker, and a philosopher who played."

If you take the time to read any of Mattie's books, you can't help but come away believing that he was a special messenger, illuminated by wisdom, love, and grace, whose brief life on earth reminds us that even in suffering one can find joy and peace.

The Sublime

Deep down, you knew the day would come, that day when something would happen that would take you completely by surprise, pushing you onto a new path, in a new direction, toward an unknown destination. On that day, you became a stranger in a strange land, a wanderer in the desert, trying to make sense of what makes no sense and trying to find purpose in what is empty of purpose. You walked unfamiliar roads with shattered assumptions of how life was supposed to be—and, in particular, how your life was meant to be. Every ordeal experienced—every fear faced, every desire thwarted, every dragon encountered—became a mirror into your soul, reflecting back who you really are, of what you are really made, and of what you are really capable. That awareness made you realize which beliefs and habits you would need to release and which new ways of thinking and behaving you would need to acquire. You understood that whatever answers you learned about your life and the reasons for your journey, mystery lay at its heart.

You are not supposed to live a comfortable life, not if you wish to live fully and love deeply. Not if you wish to ever— even just once in your lifetime—experience what is called "the Sublime." The author of *The Hunchback of Notre Dame,* Victor Hugo, looked beyond the narrow definition of the word "sublime" (something awe-inspiring in its beauty and perfection) and understood its even richer, more profound meaning. In his definition, sublime meant: "a combination of the grotesque and the beautiful." Quasimodo, the deformed hero in Hugo's epic, epitomized those qualities. If you think about it, "a combination of the grotesque and the beautiful" also epitomizes the experiences in your life. You only have to look at the news of the day to see that the world is full of stories of love that fill your heart and stories of horror that break it. Both agony and ecstasy are part of love. The more ecstasy you experience in your beloved, the more agony you will experience if your beloved leaves you whether through abandonment or death. That is the secret bargain we all make when we offer our hearts. Live long enough, you will find the joy of love followed by the pain of loss. It is by nurturing gratitude for having experienced profound love that you can bear profound pain. In doing so, the pain becomes a bittersweet reminder of exquisite beauty, and the entire experience becomes . . . sublime.

The Seven Insights

There comes a point in your transformational journey when you understand your life's progression—its hopes and heartaches, its joys and injustices—in an entirely new way. You then have a choice: allow fear to close your heart to new experiences or allow inner peace to open your heart to more of them.

The Illumination is both a state of mind and a state of being. It is fueled by an ever-expanding set of insights that help you to live your life with a greater sense of awe, appreciation, and adventure. Learning all of the insights is impossible in one lifetime. But here are seven worth considering.

1. Your higher states of consciousness are achieved through painful, transformative events.
2. Your thoughts, words, and deeds have a ripple effect.
3. Your journey is of primary importance—the outcome is secondary.
4. Your destiny is co-created.
5. Your trust in whatever happens can lead to something good.

6. Your invitation to what you allow in is determined by the emotional resistance you give out.
7. Your center of peace, joy, and love emanates from within.

1. A Higher Consciousness Is Powerful

After a transformation, you will never be able to return to old ways of thinking once the new ways have taken hold. I've spoken to countless people who have experienced strange, mystical happenings that could not be explained by ordinary means: telepathy, near-death experiences, premonitions, even visions of loved ones who had passed away. How does science explain child savants who, upon hearing a complicated piano piece they had never previously heard, are able to reproduce the music in its entirety and without error?

I was in my thirties before I connected the dots about all of those mysteries. In order for those phenomena to occur, thoughts must travel and consciousness must exist beyond the brain. I now believe that the brain functions more as a filter—filtering *out* certain information so that our perceptions aren't too confusing. But for some people—psychics, mediums, savants, persons with near-death experiences, and others with mystical experiences—the brain filters *in* information not accessible to the average person.

A study by Andrew Greeley of the National Opinion Research Center at the University of Chicago asked 1,467 adults the question: "Have you ever felt that you were very close to a powerful spiritual force that seemed to lift you out of yourself?" Thirty-nine percent responded "yes" and over the following years, as many as 50 percent of respondents answered "yes" to the same question.

I have had many mystical experiences in my life. In fact, I seem to have a knack for helping people find lost objects. My success rate, while not amazing, is better than most and, simply put, is inexplicable. Once at a Christmas party a woman who had been widowed for eight years lamented how she had lost her wedding ring shortly after her husband died. The loss pained her. As she spoke, I saw her in my mind, shaking out a bedspread and sending the ring flying through the air. It rolled underneath a dresser and landed against the wall below a heating duct. I explained my vision to the woman who told me that was not possible. "I never shake out a bedspread like that and I've searched every nook and cranny of every room in my house," she said. Three months later I received a call from her daughter. She had been visiting when her mother told her what I had said about the ring. When she learned that her mother had never even bothered to take a look, she decided to look for herself. She found the ring right where I'd said it was. I still don't know how that happened but clearly *something* had happened that was not easily explained.

The regular practice of meditation can unclutter your mind and put you in touch with a greater consciousness where wisdom and Divine guidance are more readily discernible. Once you believe that consciousness exists as an outside force and that your consciousness—your existence, your awareness of being alive—can exist outside your physical body, that belief opens up more profound questions about God, spirituality, and the nature of life and death. Did you exist before you were born? If so, did you live a past life or were you a spirit? Did you choose ahead of time what lessons you wished to learn in this life? You may not find the answers, but the questions suggest the survival of consciousness after death. In that, there is hope.

2. Look for the Beauty of the Ripple Effect

When I was in grade school, I met Dr. Benjamin Ricci, who brought to light the deplorable conditions of a mental institution in Massachusetts in the 1950s. I was ten years old at the time, but I still remember Dr. Ricci's visits and the slide show he presented. I remember thinking how awful it would be if my brother or sisters had to live under those conditions. I remember wondering why grown-ups allowed such horrible conditions to exist. And I remember wondering why Dr. Ricci would speak to a class of fifth-graders about such a situation when we could do nothing. What was his purpose? Perhaps he understood that his words might have a ripple effect, though he would never know the nature, timing, or impact of that ripple effect.

Dr. Ricci had his own heroic journey that transformed not only himself and his family but the Massachusetts educational system. When I was a boy, his courage impressed me. He probably never imagined that one of those ten-year-old students would remember his story decades later. That is the mystery of ripple effects. They happen all the time. You create ripple effects and you are influenced by those that others create. You make a difference in someone's life every day. And you will make a difference in the lives of people you have yet to meet.

Consciousness exists outside our brains. Even our intentions—good or bad—have a ripple effect. In the remarkable book *Your Body Doesn't Lie*, author John Diamond shows how one's positive or negative thoughts can affect the muscle strength of an observer. Try this experiment for yourself. Have a partner stand in front of you with his or her arms extended out to the side, elbows locked. Place your hand on the wrist of the extended arm and push down. When you have pushed down an inch or two your partner is to resist and raise the arm back to the original position. (This is not a strength test. Neither of you needs to use much force.) Your partner should have no problem resisting you. Then, without your partner knowing, think of a disturbing thought and once again press down on your partner's arm. This time your partner's deltoid muscle will get weaker and he or she will be unable to keep the arm erect—or will do so but only by exerting more force than before. Thoughts are energy. Toxic thoughts create disturbances in your body—and can potentially create disturbances in the bodies of others around you.

I believe that unseen forces offer us guidance. Such received guidance is meant to create a ripple effect for reasons you may never understand. Countless people who were victimized by disease, violence, or a tragic accident created ripple effects by becoming advocates for some great cause, thereby helping others. Your journey includes your personal transformation and also the transformation of others.

3. The Journey Is Supposed to Be Difficult

Martha sat across from me, wringing her hands. "I know I should divorce Ned," she said. "But I'm afraid. It could be years before I find the right man and by then I'll be too old to start a family." Martha and Ned had seemed the perfect couple when they married four years earlier. They had the same interests, liked the same group of friends, and had shared dreams of buying a home and raising a family. She cheered him on when he became a success in his career as a stockbroker. Martha's personality—nurturing, self-sacrificing, and ever-tolerant—was a perfect counterpoint to Ned's stubborn, flash-fire angry outbursts, and a check on his growing lust for risk-taking and life in the fast lane. "He needed someone like me to keep him grounded," she said. "He had a rough childhood, both of his parents were alcoholics, and I naively believed that if I proved to him I would always be there no matter what, he would become less angry and more at peace with himself."

Their relationship became strained to the breaking point when Ned started abusing cocaine. Martha realized then that her patient, tolerant demeanor was only enabling him. "I'm thirty-six years old," she cried. "All I've ever really wanted was to have a family and raise children. If I leave him I will probably lose that chance. But if I stay and we have children, what kind of life will they have if their father abuses drugs or we eventually divorce?" She reached for a tissue to dry her eyes. "I don't know what I should do. I don't want to make the wrong decision and regret it the rest of my life."

There was no way for Martha to predict which course of action would best bring about the desired outcome. If a teacher gave the test answers to students before the exam, the students would all get perfect scores but never master the subject matter. They would also never master life skills such as prioritizing time, persevering through difficulty, overcoming bad habits, avoiding distractions, and seeing projects through to the end. Martha's true transformation began when she accepted that truth. It continued when she took a clear stand with Ned about his drug abuse.

If your heroic journey involves very little struggle, it isn't a true journey. Heroic journeys knock you down, they test you. Transformation involves an intense, personal struggle and the release of the desires, habits, beliefs, or fears that are holding you back. In the aftermath, you will understand that the lessons learned—often painfully—are a necessary part of your soul's continual growth.

4. Your Destiny Has a Co-Creator

In August of 2001, I received a phone call from my good friend, Vinnie. Deliriously happy, Vinnie shouted into the phone, "Paul, I got the job!" Unemployed for nearly a year, Vinnie was calling me from New York City, describing the stunning view. He called me from his spectacular new office on the sixty-seventh floor that looked out over city waterways and the Statue of Liberty. Barely a month later, Vinnie, swearing at himself, woke up in a panic. He had forgotten to set his alarm and overslept. Always a hard worker and dedicated employee, he had stayed late at the office the night before; now he was a half-hour late for work.

The morning Vinnie was late for work by a mere half-hour was September eleventh, the morning of the terrorist attacks on the World Trade Center, the site of his new office. Had Vinnie arrived on time he probably would have died.

You are never completely in charge of your destiny. When your life is in upheaval you feel out of control, striving to regain control. At the beginning of a true transformational journey you will discover that you are in many ways helpless, and so you surrender. In that surrender, you open yourself up to receive guidance and to change aspects of yourself—attitudes, beliefs, behaviors—that must change if you are to move forward in your life and grow in wisdom.

Your personal changes do not tell the whole story. How did your life get turned upside down in a specific way, at a specific time? You had little or no option to choose many of the givens of your life. You didn't choose your family or the place where you grew up. You didn't entirely determine who you would meet, who would become a friend or lover. Had you grown up in a different place your life could be different. You chose a job but someone had to first choose you for that job. You probably chose the city in which to reside based upon where your job was located or where a friend or partner wanted to live. Had you chosen a different job, a different college, and a different hobby—or simply declined a party invitation—you might never have met the person who is now your best friend, your spouse, or your partner.

You decide one day to take the scenic route home from work and get seriously injured in a car accident—or you unknowingly avoided the car accident you would have experienced had you taken your usual route home. Whether it is fate, happenstance, or Divine intervention, things happen in your life over which you have no control. Your destiny is not entirely in your hands. How you respond to life events is within your range of control, but even then not always completely in your control. Your past experiences, your role models, your education, and your income are just a few of the factors that can either obstruct or enhance your ability to control or cope. Should you become seriously ill, you can choose a physician and a treatment plan for your recovery, but that recovery may depend on the skill of that physician and the limitations of your health insurance plan.

At its core, your journey of transformation is a process of letting go. You let go so that you can allow a co-creator to work alongside you and fill the places in yourself that were emptied. You receive inspired thoughts when you release pre-existing beliefs. But your ego does not sit comfortably with a co-creator. It prefers total control. It tolerates sharing but only as a means to an end, and that end is always greater control. To peacefully—and joyfully—exist alongside a co-creator makes your ego feel weak, so it refuses to consider that we are all connected to all people, all living things, and a Divine presence. Your ego confuses humility with humiliation and surrender with helplessness. It resists the efforts of a co-creator it does not fully understand or trust. Your ego assumes it knows best. When you refuse to accept the realities of your situation or the limits of your knowledge and skills, you close yourself off to guidance. You may think you are getting what you need, but you are not getting what you *really* need. More often than not, you will simply experience more heartache and turmoil. When you repeatedly find yourself banging your head against a wall, your ego has taken charge. Your ego overlooks the fact that you always have a co-creator. Will that co-creator be a constructive force or a destructive force? Ego-dominated attitudes and actions cause a domino effect, creating more chaos for yourself and others and leading to bad decisions.

5. Good Things Will Still Happen

When you have been betrayed by family or friends or battered by tragic and unfair events, no one can blame you for being less than trusting that good things can happen or for failing to believe that God has a wonderful plan for you. Fear and mistrust are often the constant companions of anyone who has been traumatized. The journey of transformation is about releasing some of your old attitudes. Real trust is not the belief that all will work out as you hope. It is not a denial of harsh realities. It is not blind faith in authority. It is a larger trust that whatever happens, something good will follow. Like Martin Luther King Jr., who didn't live long enough to see the fruits of his journey, you may never witness that greater good that unfolds. What you do witness may not be what you would choose—it is not what you think is best—but you trust in its eventual goodness.

A person with a deeper sense of trust is wise enough to know that definitions of "good" and "bad" depend upon the limited perspective of time and one's vantage point. We reveal the better side when we participate in an outpouring of love and support for others affected by a great calamity, such as a flood or earthquake. Pain and suffering often bring forth love and compassion, and a ripple effect. So, what exactly is "bad," after all? It is often those people who seem to have everything who eventually realize they have nothing. If you lost everything—your money, your health, your family, your possessions—what would sustain you? That is a question Joseph Campbell believes all of us should ponder. We would buckle under the weight of such a devastating loss, but would we survive? What would sustain us? One answer is this; that we trust that our life still has purpose and that something greater exists beyond this earthly life.

If you regret something you did and say "I should have changed my ways years ago, then none of this would have happened!" you are missing the bigger picture. You don't know what would have happened had you made changes sooner. You can't change one aspect of your history without affecting everything that happens. Don't be worried about how long it took to learn a lesson. Had you made the changes you wished, you might not exist today. If you weren't able to learn a certain lesson before now, you weren't ready to learn it. It's as simple as that. No advice, however wise, is useful until the learner is open enough to hear it, experienced enough to understand it, and courageous enough to act on it. It is better to trust that things unfold in their own time for reasons we do not always understand.

The universe is perfect and its perfection is beyond our understanding. It is alive with consciousness that takes notice of every passing thought, every drop of rain, and every act of peace or war, love or hate in the world. We can't possibly understand the deepest reasons why things happen the way they do, but we never stop trying. Failing in that effort, we fall back on blaming ourselves for not being careful, blaming others for not being kind, blaming the universe for not being fair, or blaming God for not being godly. The only real solution we have to achieve peace is to trust.

A message in a bottle is tossed into the open sea. Sometimes you are that bottle; adrift in the sea, uncertain where you will end up but destined to end up somewhere for an unclear purpose. Sometimes you are the message; offering guidance by virtue of the story of your journey. Despite the losses you've suffered or the love you've secured, you can take comfort in trusting that there is always something more, always something good.

6. Invite Peace Into Your Life

"I'm in recovery," Angela flatly said to me. "It's a lifelong process." When she was a child, her stepfather had sexually abused Angela for years. Her mother said she was never aware of what was going on, but Angela never believed her. "I feel betrayed by both of them," she said. She had been in therapy for years with another counselor and told me she had made tremendous progress in her recovery. "I used to blame myself for what happened. I assumed I was the bad person. I felt dirty. Now I realize my stepfather was the bad person, not me."

Despite her progress, Angela still felt unsettled. Freed from self-blame, she was now imprisoned by rage. She raged at what had happened to her and at her ongoing mistrust of others. This made romantic relationships difficult. "Trying to get close to someone is, for me, like trying to pet an alligator. All of my relationships have ended in disaster."

"You're afraid of intimacy, you fear getting hurt, you take things personally, and you don't trust easily," I said. "There are basically three types of people who would be attracted to you."

"Okay. Tell me," she said.

"The first type would be the rescuer, the knight in shining armor who wants to prove to you that love will conquer all. Problems arise when you resist his efforts, doubt his motives, and push him away."

"That's happened already," she said.

I continued. "The second type is similar to the first. He is basically insecure and would be afraid that if you recovered from your past you might leave him. He needs you to stay dependent on him."

"That's happened, too," she said. "Do you have a crystal ball or something?"

"The third type is just the opposite. He has such low self-esteem that he needs you in his life in order for him to survive emotionally. He will do whatever you ask. He's just grateful he has someone that wants him. You can easily control him— which makes you feel safer—but you will grow weary of his neediness and dependency."

"You just described my current relationship," Angela said. "No wonder I'm miserable."

Angela was stuck, but she didn't know why. Holding her parents responsible for their actions was a sign of progress, but her level of bitterness toward them was now overwhelming her. On one level, blaming her stepfather, who had indeed abused her, and blaming her mother, who had not protected her, makes sense. But blaming, however justified, had become an obstacle to her inner peace. Her belief that recovery is a lifelong process is a common belief among trauma victims and addicts. If you are recovering from a wound, not yet healed, and are convinced that recovery is lifelong, can you ever then be healed?

"What would it mean if you finally and completely recovered?" I asked. "How would that change your life?"

"I suppose I'd feel happy and free," she said. "I wouldn't be bitter. I don't know if I could ever get close to my parents again. Actually, I would never get close to them again. If I did, my stepfather would think he got away with what he did."

"So holding on to bitterness and failing in relationships is like holding up a sign to your parents that says 'See what you've done!'" I said.

Angela wanted to overcome the impact of abuse but didn't want to let her parents off the hook. That resistance perpetuated her anger and caused her to seek out relationships that were bound to fail.

"I don't want to forgive them," Angela said.

"You don't have to if you don't want to," I said. "But can you stop shaking your fist at what happened and simply accept that it did happen? Can you step away from judging it and just accept it?"

When Angela emotionally accepted what had happened to her, she became open to other ways of thinking, feeling, and behaving. It may seem hard to believe, but the ego loves unhappiness since it needs something to fight against. It needs you to resist in order for it to exist. It needs you to be unhappy, angry, resentful, guilty, or worried so that it can offer you alternatives and remind you how much safer you are with your ego in your life. It looks for problems. When you try to talk yourself out of a worry and reassure yourself things will be okay, it whispers in your ear, "But what if you're wrong?" Once you transcend your ego, transcend fear and personal desires, you can peacefully coexist with acceptance, faith, trust, love, and gratitude. Higher-self virtues resist nothing but create inner peace. Your ego loses power and control when you experience inner peace. It pesters you to replace acceptance with resistance, trust with doubt, and gratitude with entitlement.

All forms of judgment reside in your ego. It's hard to imagine going through a normal day without making judgments. It is how you navigate through your world. But judgments complicate your ability to find inner peace. Your ego is very useful for solving problems of a practical nature, but only your higher self can deal with problems of a spiritual nature.

If you place your ego, your lower self, in charge of helping you through grief, it will look for ways to make you feel unsafe, insecure, or angry, always reminding you of the injustice of your loss. It wants you to hold someone accountable. It will stir up fears and desires. At best it may numb your pain, keeping you preoccupied, getting you to pretend that the loss wasn't so painful after all.

If you place your higher self in charge of your grief, you will still feel the sadness of loss—but you will also experience the beauty within sadness and the love within loss.

7. Peace Lives in Your Center

Who are you? If you answer with a list of personality traits, interests, skills, habits, tendencies, or potentials, I say you are not that. Those are qualities. A leaf on a tree may be green. The color green is a quality but the leaf's essence is not green. If a quality is also its essence, "A leaf is green" and "Green is a leaf" would make perfect sense. But the concept of green does not equal the concept of leaf. Something can be green and not be a leaf. You may be beautiful but the concept of beauty is not defined entirely by you. Other people (and things) not you are also beautiful.

So, now who are you? You are not your body. Your body changes constantly. The body you had as a child no longer exists. Not one cell of that body exists today. Those cells died and new cells were created. But "you" still exist. You didn't die when your cells died. You exist apart from your body. So what is the essence of "you"? It's a difficult question but one you should continue asking yourself.

When you are agitated about something, ask yourself "*Is this a peaceful thought? A joyful thought? A loving thought?*" If you answer "No," then ask also if you wish to change that thought. Do you take things personally? If others disagree with your political or religious opinions, do you take offense or get defensive? Does rejection make you think you are unworthy or does it make you think that the person who rejected you is unworthy? Why does someone have to be labeled? Does a label bring inner peace? It's understandable to be sad or hurt if you've been rejected, or disappointed if you didn't achieve some sought-after goal. But if you can accept the reality of your situation without the added judgment that you or someone else is at fault, you can feel more peaceful.

You cannot say no to experience. You can't even say no to transformation. It will happen with or without you. As you travel along your journey, here are some questions to answer:

- Will you be transformed in the direction of your higher self or your lower self?
- Will you accept that your journey is made more arduous by resistance and more sublime by acceptance?
- Will you be mentally calm so as to notice inspired guidance, like the ripple of a leaf falling upon a calm lake?
- Will you choose to let go of unhelpful beliefs and old habits that no longer serve you?
- Will you choose to believe in goodness when your mind has doubts?
- Will you choose to believe that your existence serves a Divine purpose that you may never comprehend?
- Will you choose to be kind, grateful, and forgiving when you have reason to be the opposite?
- Will you act in alignment with love, peace, joy, or gratitude instead of fear or desire?

The Journey Continues

The pointed arrow of loss and grief has pierced you. Eventually you realized that the arrow's point—sharp as it is—is forged not of metal but of life itself. The impacts made you realize this: In the end what counts is to live fully, love passionately, create soulfully, and endure gratefully. You will then know what it is to be fully alive and human.

There will be other journeys. In every life there are losses and injuries, broken hearts and broken dreams. You now find yourself on a new road, facing a future you can't predict. And you come face to face with a powerful adversary challenging you. When you meet him on the road, this time, welcome him. Embrace him. That adversary is your friend. He is you.

CONCLUSION

Goodbyes Are Not Forever

"I will love the light for it shows me the way;
Yet I will endure the darkness
for it shows me the stars."

—OG MANDINO

Finding Peace Together

It was Monday morning and high school classes were canceled. There had been a huge blizzard overnight. But my normal excitement was short-lived when the phone rang. My dad answered, and from the expression on his face I knew something terrible had happened. His voice cracked when all he could manage to say was "Tony?" The person calling was my sister Ann. Tony was her youngest child, a month shy of his second birthday. What seemingly began as a mild cold had overnight filled his lungs with infection. Tony died from acute pneumonia in my sister Ann's arms on the way to the hospital.

Eight months later while raking the fall leaves, Tony's dad noticed something tangled in the leaf litter. He picked it up, brushing it off, and was astonished to see that it was one of Tony's tiny leather dress shoes. Lost, it had spent an entire year hidden among the leaves. My sister, thrilled to find this bittersweet reminder of her love and loss, tucked it away for safekeeping.

The years following Tony's passing became an emotional struggle for my sister and her husband. They had different ways of grieving. Eventually their marriage ended, their house was sold, and my sister spent many years moving from one apartment to another. During one of those moves she discovered that Tony's shoe, so carefully saved, was nowhere to be found. My sister's final move was to Seattle to be near her now grown daughter and her grandchildren.

It was now the spring of 2011 and forty winters had passed. My sister was visiting the East Coast and my wife and I met her in Vermont, where she would be spending time with her dear friend, Ted. Ted owned a huge, cavernous warehouse that was filled to the brim with musty books, engine parts, stacks of wood, and enough outdated, worn furniture to furnish dozens of homes. Coincidentally, my son Luke was getting ready to move out of our house and into his first apartment. When Ted heard that, he graciously invited us to choose whatever furniture we could fit into our van for Luke to take to his new home. We spent an hour searching until finally, tucked under a mountain of furniture, I spied the perfect piece for my son's first apartment—a sturdy end-table that looked to be in great condition. My sister turned to look at my find, walked over to it, paused, and ran her hand along its top as if caressing a long-lost love. Turning back to me with a soft smile she told me how delighted and astonished she was at my choice. The table, she said, had once belonged to her. She had given it to Ted decades earlier.

Amazing! Of all the pieces of furniture to choose, how did I select that one piece that had belonged to my sister? We all laughed together as I looked it over and checked to see if the drawer opened and closed properly. Everything was fine and we hoisted it into my van for the ride home. Weeks later as I lifted the table to move it, I heard a soft rattling sound from inside the drawer. Opening it up, I saw cradled in the well of the drawer a tiny leather shoe, *the perfect size for a toddler . . .*

"You found the shoe!" my stunned sister said when I called her in Seattle. That day I mailed her Tony's baby shoe. It was a very special delivery.

Goodbyes are not forever. And random events, perhaps, are not random at all.

The Lost and the Found

It is fitting that this book about *loss* would end with a story about what was *found*. And it's ironic that a book about walking the heroic journey through life's tribulations while seeking inner peace . . . ends with a story about a shoe.

Those with a purely scientific mind would argue that the coincidences in my shoe story can occur within the realm of chance and that meaningful coincidences need not have mystical origins. After all, someone must win a one-in-ten-million lottery. Despite my scientific training, I've had far too many one-in-ten-million experiences in my life to believe they were all pure chance. What if Tony's dad had not found his son's baby shoe among the leaves? What if my sister had not placed the tiny shoe in the table drawer? What if she had not given the table to Ted? What if my son wasn't about to move into his first apartment or had no need for furniture? What if my wife and I had not met up with my sister in Vermont? What if Ted had not generously offered us furniture? What if I had not chosen that particular table? What if *any* of those things had not occurred? Well then, there would be no story of the shoe.

What an extraordinary set of circumstances! Was Tony's shoe *meant* to be found? My life's work as a psychologist and countless personal experiences that have crossed the boundary from credible to incredible have convinced me that goodbyes are not forever and that impossible coincidences are more commonplace than we ever imagined. Perhaps that has been your experience, too. If not, once you discover the Four Paths of Transformation to inner peace you will understand what I mean.

Your heroic journey to inner peace is not just challenging. Sometimes it will seem downright amazing. Everyone embarks on journeys unasked for; journeys that seem so painful at times that they forge our very hearts and souls anew, as if our hearts and souls never before existed. As I've traveled my own journeys, I have accepted the loss of my loved ones. I have been inspired to pursue a quest for greater understanding of the Divine. I have trusted that what happens in my life, however difficult or challenging, can still serve me in some way. And I have tried to act with compassion toward myself and others. As a result I sleep more easily, walk more humbly, smile more readily, love more warmly, feel gratitude more fully—and experience more often what so many yearn to experience: a peaceful heart.

May your own journey lead you to these places of peace.

INDEX